Meet the Cat Family!

Part 1: The International Lineages

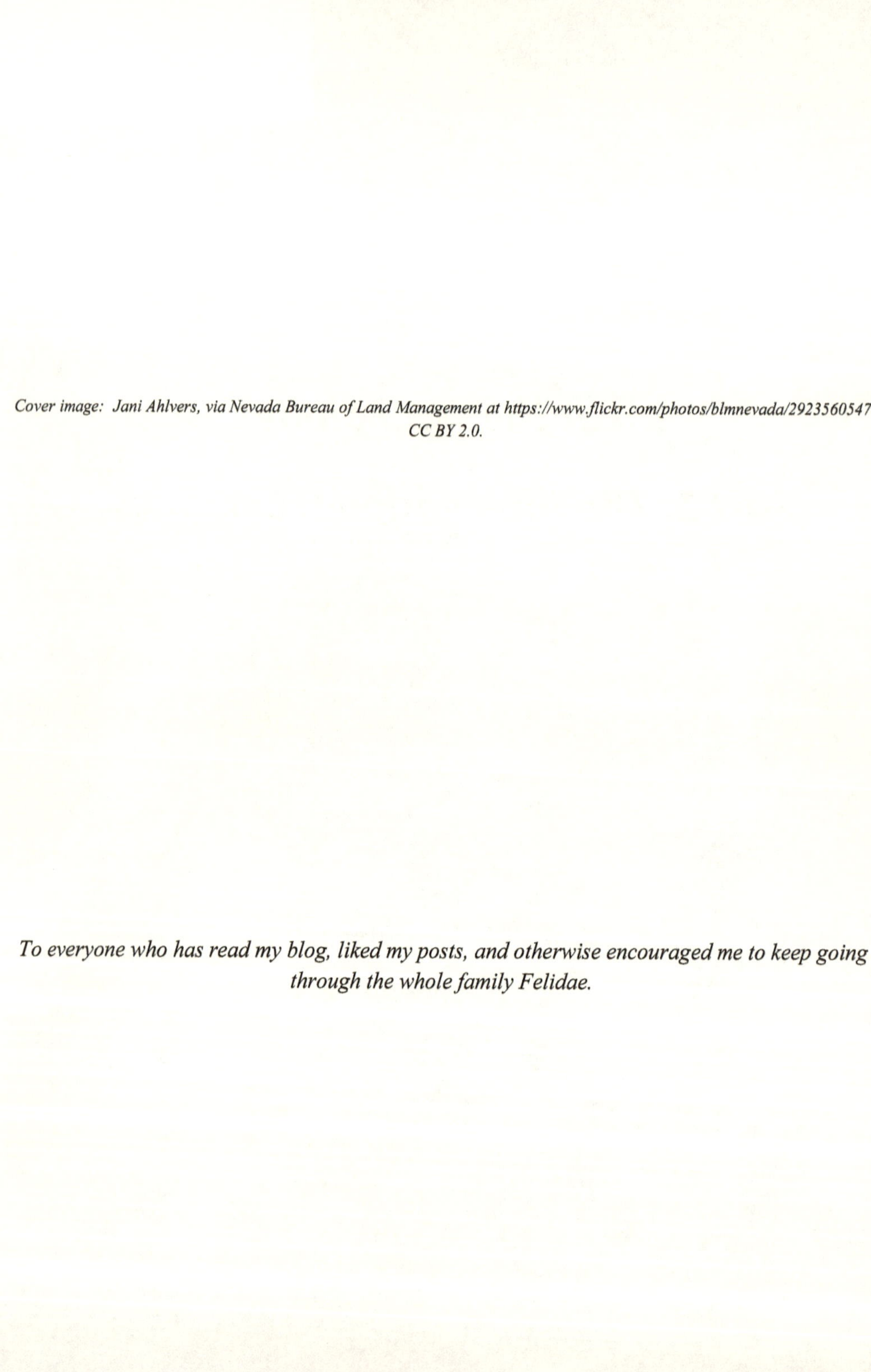

Cover image: Jani Ahlvers, via Nevada Bureau of Land Management at https://www.flickr.com/photos/blmnevada/29235605474, CC BY 2.0.

To everyone who has read my blog, liked my posts, and otherwise encouraged me to keep going through the whole family Felidae.

Contents

Preface

This book is about 4 transcontinental feline lineages -- big cats, the puma and its relatives, lynxes, and wildcats. Altogether, we're going to look at 17 different cats.

In a sense, though, all members of family Felidae are international.

Fossil and molecular studies suggest that their ancestors originated in Eurasia tens of millions of years ago. As time passed, those prehistoric cats gradually spread across the northern continents and down into Africa.

The southern continents were surrounded by water back in those days, and cats could not reach them until plate tectonics re-connected the two American continents through the Panama Isthmus a few million years ago.

Then sabercats and ancestors of modern cats moved into South America and took their place at the top of the food chain there, too.

Of course, scientists want to know how this all played out, but they don't have much evidence to work with.

They have been able to model cat the family's ancient travels with the help of both fossils and molecular DNA markers. But, as of this writing, there is still no consensus on exactly how cats evolved and how they got to where they're found today.

This modeling can' t explain why some lineages, like the bay cat's, stayed in one place (Asia, for the bay cat) while other lineages -- those we will meet in this book -- wandered far and wide.

But what's a lineage, anyway?

Think of it as a family tree branch with various cats sitting on it:

- Big cats are on the ***Panthera*** branch.

- Cheetahs, believe it or not, share a branch with the ***puma*** and Latin America's jaguarundi (a small cat, not related to jaguars).

- The ***lynx*** group, which includes bobcats, has a branch of its own.

- Yes, there is a "Domestic Cat" branch, too (it's sometimes called ***Felis***). In this book, we'll just look at Felis cats that became world travelers -- the rest are local to either Asia or Africa.

In lieu of personally tracking down every species, I've used information from the Cat Specialist Group at http://www.catsg.org/ and the International Union for the Conservation of Nature (also known as the IUCN -- it's responsible for the Red List of endangered animals and plants) at https://www.iucnredlist.org/, as well as a host of other reliable sources that you can check in the reference section at the end of this book.

For which cats belong to which lineage, I have arbitrarily selected two different sources: a widely cited paper by Johnson *et al*. in 2006 and another one by Nyakatura and Bininda-Emonds in 2012.

The two teams agree on the general outline of the cat family tree but differ on some details. Fortunately, since we're just skimming the surface here, those disagreements don't affect our look at international cats.

After all, this isn't a textbook or research paper.

It is just your introduction to some of the world's most beautiful and mysterious predators.

References:

1. **Cat Specialist Group.** *http://www.catsg.org/*

2. **International Union for the Conservation of Nature.** *https://www.iucnredlist.org/*

3. **Johnson, W. E.; Eizirik, E.; Pecon-Slattery, J.; Murphy, W. J.; and others.** *2006. The Late Miocene Radiation of Modern Felidae: A Genetic Assessment. Science, 311: 73-77.*

4. **Nyakatura, K., and Bininda-Emonds, O. R. P.** *2012. Updating the evolutionary history of Carnivora (Mammalia): a new species-level supertree complete with divergence time estimates, BMC Biology, 10: 12.*

The big cat lineage

Lions

Benh Lieu Song, https://www.flickr.com/photos/blieusong/7233890820, CC BY-SA 2.0

Name: The English word "lion" comes from similar-sounding Latin and Ancient Greek terms for this beautiful big cat.

Its scientific name is *Panthera leo*.

Until recently, there were two recognized subspecies:

1. African lions (*Panthera leo leo*)

2. Asiatic lions (*P. leo persica*), which are only found wild today in one small park in India

However, lion taxonomy is definitely a work in progress. Leo's list of subspecies and their names will probably change over time.

Lineage: Panthera.

Outstanding Features:

1. **Mane and tail tassel**: Lions start to grow a yellow, brown, or reddish brown mane at around age 3-1/2 years; by age 5 or 6, it's complete and will continue to darken and thicken as the lion ages. The mane on Asiatic lions is less prominent than the African lion's mane. (*Cat Specialist Group*; *Sunquist and Sunquist*) Tail tassels first appear on both lions and lionesses when they're about 5-1/2 months old. No one is quite sure why these unique features evolved. Perhaps a lion's mane show his physical condition to potential mates and rivals, while tail tassels might be useful visual signals during a stalk or at other times where it's important to be quiet.

Lionesses have a tail tassel, too. (Image: Tambako the Jaguar , https://www.flickr.com/photos/tambako/21715608974 CC BY-ND 2.0)

2. **The pride**: Lions are the only cat species known to be *this* social. Related lionesses form the core, averaging 4 or 5 per pride in India's Gir National Park and up to 18 out on the Serengeti. (*Sunquist and Sunquist*) Males come and go (2 to 6 per pride in Gir, on average, and 1 to 7 in Serengeti prides, per Sunquist and Sunquist), with an average tenure of 24 to 36 months before another lion or coalition of young males moves in to take over the pride. (*Cat Specialist Group*)

oNabby/Shutterstock

3. **ROAR!!!** This mighty sound may be unique to lions. Tigers, leopards, and jaguars certainly sound like they're roaring,

but according to Kitchener *et al.* (2010), sonograms show that only the lion has a complete structured call series. Here is a YouTube compilation of lions roaring: https://www.youtube.com/watch?v=uFcZhH_wFbs .

Data: This information is from the Cat Specialist Group, except where noted. There's a wide number spread in each category because lions are much bigger than lionesses.

- **Weight**: 240 to 600 pounds (African); 240 to 420 pounds (Asiatic).

- **Height at the shoulder**: 3 to 4 feet (*Sunquist and Sunquist*)

- **Body length**: 4-1/2 to 8 feet.

- **Tail length**: 2 to a little over 3 feet.

- **Coat**: Adults have solid-colored short fur that ranges in color from light tan to silvery gray, yellowish red, or even dark brown. Cubs often have spots that usually fade with time. The adult cat's underside is generally a paler version of its overall coat color. (*Sunquist and Sunquist*) White lions aren't albinos; they just have a genetic mutation -- here are more details about that: http://messybeast.com/genetics/lions-white.htm.

- **Litter size**: 1 to 4 cubs.

Eric Kilby , https://www.flickr.com/photos/ekilby/20842 583564 CC BY-SA 2.0

Where found in the wild:

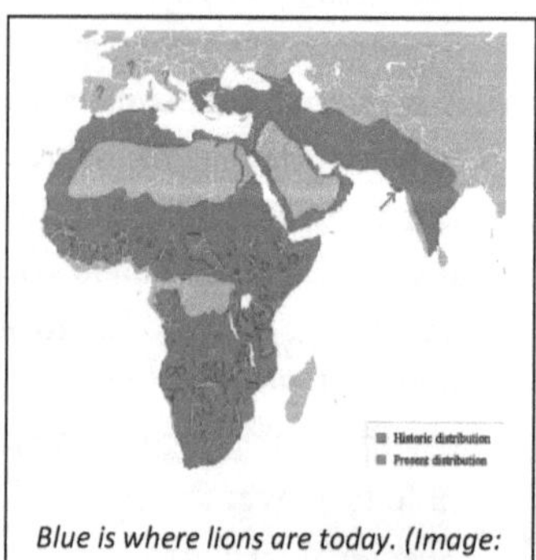

Blue is where lions are today. (Image: Tommyknocker via Wikimedia , https://commons.wikimedia.org/wiki/ File:Lion_distribution.png)

Historic records show that *P. leo* once roamed across all of Africa and much of Europe, the Middle East, and southwestern Asia.

Today lions live south of the Sahara, with more than half of them found in conservation areas. The only known wild population of Asiatic lions, about 400 individuals, inhabit Gir Park and its environs in Gujarat State, India. (*Cat Specialist Group; Macdonald et al., 2010a*)

Habitat:

- **Range of environments:** Lions generally are

very adaptable and have been observed from the coast all the way up to some 14,000 feet in the mountains. Most live on savanna lands that provide some cover and support numerous prey animals.

- **Prey base:** Like many cats, lions are generalists and will eat anything they come across. Given a choice, they'll take hoofed animals, like antelope and wildebeests, in the 200- to 600-pound class. This works out especially well for the coordinated hunting style of lionesses, but lions, despite their reputation for laziness, can also hunt well. After all, they must support themselves until they get a pride of their own!

- **Example of guild:** The African large predator guild also includes leopards, spotted hyenas, cheetahs, and the African wild dog. Most of the time, the pride is in charge, but sometimes other predators -- particularly hyenas -- gang up on lionesses at a kill and may even steal it unless a lion is nearby to drive them off.

Gudkov Andrey/Shutterstock

Red-list status:

- **African lions**: Vulnerable. IUCN assessment: https://www.iucnredlist.org/species/15951/115130419

- **Asiatic lions**: Endangered. IUCN assessment: https://www.iucnredlist.org/species/15952/5327221

Tigers

Tambako the Jaguar, https://www.flickr.com/photos/tambako/9876813033 CC BY-ND 2.0

Name: Ancient Greeks reportedly borrowed the word "tigris" from some unknown source and used it for both the Middle Eastern river and this beautiful striped cat. Over time, the cat's name has turned into "tiger."

Its scientific name still reflects that historic term: *Panthera tigris*.

Tigers have many common names, based on where they're found:

Malayan tiger (upper left): Jean, CC BY 2.0, https://www.flickr.com/photos/7326810@N08/18913337416; **Amoy tiger** (upper center): Wikimedia, CC BY-SA 1.0, https://commons.wikimedia.org/wiki/File:Panthera_tigris_amoyensis.jpg; **Amur/Siberian tiger** (with cubs) (upper right): mcamcamca, CC BY-SA 2.0, https://www.flickr.com/photos/27461854@N04/3957681113; **Bengal Tiger** (lower left): Derrick Brutel, CC BY-SA 2.0, https://www.flickr.com/photos/143951935@N07/27466438332; **Indochinese tigers** (lower center): Doug Beckers, CC BY-SA 2.0, https://www.flickr.com/photos/dougbeckers/4547769859; and **Sumatran tiger** (lower right): Bernard Spragg, NZ, https://www.flickr.com/photos/volvob12b/9122811106 public domain

Yes, they all look very much alike. There are some genetic differences, but the boffins are still debating formal tiger subspecies names.

Lineage: Panthera.

Jean-Pierre Dalbera
https://www.flickr.com/photos/dalbera/310603
00228 CC BY 2.0

Outstanding Features:

1. Individual Amur and Bengal tigers are the **biggest cats in the world**. However, there is quite a range of sizes. Some tigers living near the Equator are smaller than African lions!

2. **Stripes!** Some experts suspect that stripes evolved to hide tigers in tall grass, but more research suggests that this isn't the case. (*Allen et al.*) One study found that stripes have the right "spatial frequency" to conceal a stalking

tiger's movements from its prey. (Here is more information about spatial frequency: http://www.ucalgary.ca/pip369/mod4/spatial/frequency1)

3. Bengal tigers have the **longest fangs in the modern cat family.** (*Heske*)

4. Tigers may have the **shortest developmental branch of any member of the cat family**. (*Cho et al.; Culver et al.; Haslam and Petraglia; Williams*) In plain English, their genetic "reset button" has been hit a few times over the last 100,000 years. Why? Apart from brushes with extinction thanks to human activities over the last couple of centuries, no one really knows what happened, although plenty of hypotheses are currently on the table.

Data: These are from the Cat Specialist Group unless otherwise noted. As you'll see, tiger size varies a lot from place to place.

- **Weight**: 165 to 716 pounds.

- **Height at the shoulder**: 2.3 to 4 feet. (*Sunquist and Sunquist; Wikipedia*)

- **Body length**: 5 to 7.6 feet.

- **Tail length**: 3 to 3.6 feet.

- **Coat**: Rusty red to yellowish-orange background color, with pure black or brownish stripes. Coat patterns are unique, including markings on the side of the tiger's face, identify individuals. All tigers have straight dark lines over their eyes. The tail has dark rings and a black tip. Underparts are usually white. Male tigers, especially on Sumatra, have a prominent ruff (not a mane). Reports of melanistic (all-black) tigers haven't been verified, but blue-eyed tigers with light sepia stripes on a white background are well known. (*Ewer; Heptner and Sludskii; Kitchener et al., 2010; Schneider et al.; Xu et al.; Wikipedia*)

White tigers are a thing, too. (Image: Jack Fiallos, https://www.flickr.com/photos/erlingfiallos/500 979330 CC BY 2.0)

- **Vocals**: Most of the typical feline sounds except purring. Along with clouded leopards, snow leopards, and jaguars, tigers "chuff" (another word for this friendly feline greeting is "prusten"). They also grunt sociably, but when feeling tense tigers moan (you can listen to it here: https://youtu.be/_UbDeqPdUek). In terms of roaring, Kitchener *et al.*

(2010) report that tigers only do some parts of the full call that lions perform. (*Christiansen; Sunquist and Sunquist; Wikipedia*)

- **Average litter size**: 1 to 5 (typically, per Ewer, 2 to 3).

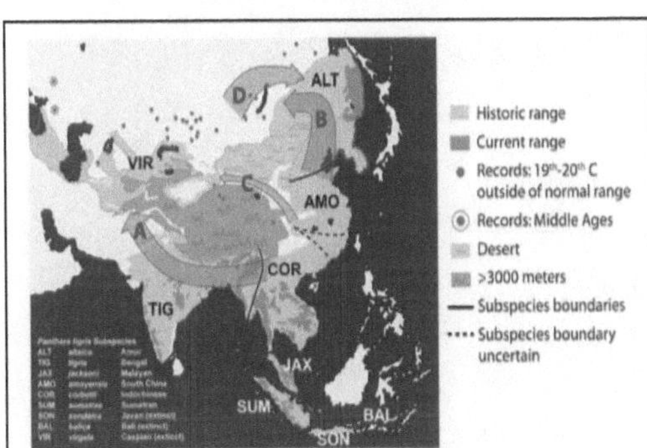

Figure 1: Driscoll, C. A.; Yamaguchi, N.; Bar-Gal, G. K.; Roca, A. L.; and others. 2009 Mitochondrial phylogeography Illuminates the origin of the extinct Caspian Tiger and Its relationship to the Amur tiger. PLoS ONE 4(1): e4125. https://journals.plos.org/plosone/article?id=10.1371/journal.pone.0004125 *Public domain*

Where found in the wild:

This image is from an open-access scientific publication.

Tigers used to be in the tan areas; now they' re only in the pink areas.

Habitat:

- **Range of environments:** Tigers prefer open woodlands, but they're flexible enough to handle everything from Siberian snow country to coastal mangrove swamps in the Ganges River delta and some of Indonesia's equatorial rain forests. As long as there is water around and not too much snow in winter, tigers are good to go.

- **Prey base:** Water attracts the large, hoofed plant-eaters like deer and wild boar that tigers probably evolved to hunt. A single cat can eat at least 50 of these 200-pound-plus animals each year.

- **Example of guild:** In Asia, tigers, leopards, and dholes (a wild dog species) are often top carnivores. Tigers don't always have it all their own way, though. While some studies show that leopards and dholes avoid tigers (*Steinmetz et al.*), in areas where prey is limited there may be intense competition (*Wang and MacDonald*).

Ondrej Prosicky/Shutterstock

Red-list status:

Endangered to **Critically Endangered**, depending on region. See the IUCN assessment at https://www.iucnredlist.org/species/15955/50659951 and the Cat Specialist Group web page at http://www.catsg.org/index.php?id=124 for more information.

Leopards

Tony Hisgett, https://www.flickr.com/photos/37804979@N00/48225242392 CC BY 2.0

Name: The word "leopard" might have come about because of an old misconception that this was a combination of lion (*leos*, in Ancient Greek) and "pard⍰ -- a term used back in the day for what we now know are several different species of spotted wild cats.

The leopard's scientific name is *Panthera pardus*.

There is much debate about subspecies, which isn't surprising, given how hard it is to study such an elusive animal, especially one that has so many different looks.

Lineage: Panthera.

Outstanding Features:

1. **SPOTS!!!** Each leopard has a unique pattern. There are also rosettes -- spots linked up into a ring or square. Jaguars have almost identical coats, so here is how to tell leopards and jaguars apart: the leopard's rosettes usually have pale centers; those on a jaguar have a central spot.

abxyz/Shutterstock

2. The **largest spotted cat in Asia and Africa**. Some of the smaller ones include cheetahs and servals in Africa, the Eurasian lynx, and Asia's little leopard cat.

3. The **greatest geographic range of any cat today**. Look for leopards from the Russian Far East southward across Asia and the Middle East all the way down to the tip of Africa. During the ice ages and into Neolithic times, leopards also inhabited western and central Europe.

4. The **broadest diet of <u>any</u> large hypercarnivore (not just cats)**. (*Jacobson et al.*) Hypercarnivores -- unlike bears and other omnivores -- need meat in their diet or they will die. That said, leopards eat almost anything from insects to ibexes. They've even been observed chowing down on watermelons in India! (*Sunquist and Sunquist*) As well, some develop specialized food favorites, particularly for dogs and jackals.

5. **Able to tolerate human presence better than other big cats can**. Leopards have been found living near international airport runways as well as in densely populated suburbs in India and Africa. They maintain such a low profile that no one usually knows they're there. But this, obviously, is a huge problem for both cat and people.

Data: These are from the Cat Specialist Group unless otherwise noted.

- **Weight**: 40 to 200 pounds. That's not a typo. Leopards do vary a lot across their extensive range. However, you won't typically see 40-pound and 200-pound adults of the same subspecies.

- **Body length**: 36 to 75 inches.

- **Tail length**: 20 to 40 inches.

- **Coat**: Background fur is anything from golden yellow to pale gray, with leopards near the Equator having the most intense hues. Farther north, in the land of snow and freezing temperatures, Amur leopards are light-colored and shaggy enough to be mistaken for snow leopards. On all leopards, the underparts are typically white. Spots occur everywhere, but rosettes usually appear on the back and flanks. Melanistic (all-black) leopards are the original "black panther" and most often seen in tropical forests, particularly on the island of Java and much of the Malay Peninsula. (*Cat Specialist Group; Heptner and Sludskii; Sunquist and Sunquist; Uphyrkina et al.*)

Amur leopard (Image: Tony Hisgett, https://www.flickr.com/photos/hisgett/5017707785 CC BY 2.0)

- **Vocals**: The leopard's signature sound is "sawing" (watch a wild leopard do this mating/territorial call right in front of a camera trap here: https://youtu.be/oZigyLQeAQw). Leopards also grunt, mew, snarl, spit, and hiss; their vocal folds are too large for them to purr. When among friends, leopards make a "puff" sound rather than chuffing like tigers and a few other big cats. (*Ewer; Sunquist and Sunquist*)

- **Average litter size**: 1-4 cubs; per Ewer, usually 2-3.

Where found in the wild:

The leopard's geographic range is the same as it was in the mid-18th century, **pink** on this map. Leopards now live in the **red** areas.

Modern leopard country runs from the Russian Far East south through parts of subtropical and tropical Asia, including the island of Java (but not Borneo or Sumatra), and westward through India and the Middle East, down into sub-Saharan Africa.

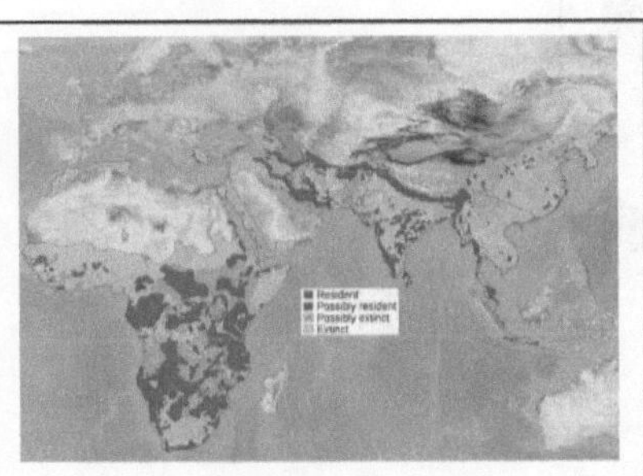

BhagyaMani via https://commons.wikimedia.org/wiki/File:Leopard_distribution.jpg#mw-jump-to-license Wikimedia, CC BY-SA 4.0

Habitat:

- **Range of environments:** Basically anything except true desert. These incredibly adaptable cats have been observed from various coastal settings all the way up to 17,000 feet in the Himalayas. They even settle in urban areas, including the outskirts of Mumbai and Johannesburg.

- **Prey base:** Leopards will take what they can get, but they prefer hoofed animals under 100 pounds and sometimes show individual food preferences, particularly for domestic dogs and other canids. Some even have a taste for porcupines!

- **Example of guild:** Africa has the most leopards today. They're found in thickets, grassland, open woods, and more densely forested environments. Out on the Serengeti, leopards keep a low profile around lions and find ways to coexist or intimidate other large predators, like cheetahs, hyenas, and various canids.

Red-list status:

Vulnerable. This may change as new information comes in, so check out conservation sites like the Cat Specialist Group at http://www.catsg.org/index.php?id=110 , the IUCN at https://www.iucnredlist.org/species/15954/102421779 , and Panthera at https://www.panthera.org/cat/leopard for the latest information.

Henrik Sommerfeld,
https://www.flickr.com/photos/henrikpalm/7555972236 CC BY 2.0

Jaguars

Tambako the Jaguar, https://www.flickr.com/photos/tambako/34809093226 CC BY-ND 2.0

Name: "Jaguar" comes to us through the Portuguese, who reportedly got it from a native South American word meaning "beast of prey."

The scientific name is *Panthera onca*.

Experts have different views on possible jaguar subspecies; to keep things simple, let's follow Kitchener *et al.* (2017) and consider the jaguar to be a single species.

Lineage: Panthera.

Outstanding Features:

1. **The only big cat in the Americas**. Mountain "lions," a/k/a cougars or pumas, don't count -- they have their own lineage. Fossils show that lions did make it to North America during the Pleistocene, and tigers might have gotten as far as Alaska. However, these two members of Panthera were gone by the end of the last ice age, leaving only the jaguar to rule the land.

Brian McKay,
https://www.flickr.com/photos/tiger_feet/3946
922593 CC BY 2.0

2. **Latin America's largest carnivore**. (*Sunquist and Sunquist*)

3. Possibly **the most powerfully built cat ever.** That includes not just tigers and lions but also every sabercat except Smilodon and a few species of Smilodon's ancestor, Megantereon! (*Turner and Antón*) As for the leopard, well, if they were sports players, the leopard would be a major-league baseball player; jaguars would own the world championship belt in every professional wrestling league. For life.

4. **The only big cat to regularly use a piercing skull bite** in addition to the typical feline killing bite to a large prey's throat or to the back of a small animal's neck. (*Cat Specialist Group*) Watch this jaguar use that power to kill and carry off a caiman (a heavily armored Amazon crocodilian): https://youtu.be/DBNYwxDZ_pA .

Data: These are from the Cat Specialist Group unless otherwise noted. As with other big cats, jaguar size varies a lot.

- **Weight**: 80 to a little over 300 pounds. The largest jaguars live near the Equator; body size gradually decreases as *P. onca* ranges farther north and south.

- **Body length**: 43 to 67 inches.

- **Tail length**: 17 to 32 inches.

*Tambako the Jaguar,
https://www.flickr.com/photos/
tambako/34306724605 CC BY-
ND 2.0*

- **Coat**: Background fur color is pale yellow to tawny brown, with spotted white fur on the cat's underparts. Melanistic (black) jaguars are relatively common, though it's a different gene mutation from the one that turns leopards black. Jaguar spots and rosettes are very similar to those of a leopard. The heftier build of a jaguar makes identification easy, but if all you have is an image, look carefully for at least one small spot inside a rosette. Jaguars usually have this; leopards have clear centers to their rosettes.

- **Vocals**: The San Diego Zoo's online jaguar page at https://animals.sandiegozoo.org/animals/jaguar describes a male's roar as "more like a bark, followed by a growl," while the female's is "a sound like a coughing roar." Besides making typical feline noises like mewing (*Wikipedia*), jaguars "chuff" among friends and family, as do tigers, snow leopards, and clouded leopards. They do not purr.

- **Average litter size**: 1 to 4 cubs, usually 2. (*Sunquist and Sunquist*)

Where found in the wild:

During recorded history, jaguars have ranged from the US states of Washington and Oregon south to Patagonia at the tip of South America, but this is no longer the case today.

The last Californian jaguar was killed in 1860. A very few are still seen in the US Southwest, mainly in Arizona, but these are probably wanderers from northern Mexico rather than part of a local breeding population. (*Cat Specialist Group*)

Most jaguars now prowl through parts of Mexico, Central America, and South America down to the Rio Negro in Argentina. Their main stronghold is in Amazonia.

Habitat:

- **Range of environments:** While jaguars have been sighted from coastal scrubland up to around 10,000 feet in the Andes, they are generally found in dense cover at elevations below 3000 feet. It doesn't have to be a rainforest -- jaguars are quite happy in a variety of habitats, even dry thorn scrub and lowland pastures with nearby forests and undergrowth.

- **Prey base:** Jaguars are generalists. More than 85 jaguar prey species have been identified, but these big cats prefer large hoofed mammals like peccaries, as well as turtles in some parts of South America -- with those strong jaws, jaguars can break through the shell and sometimes eat a small turtle whole. The cats hunt elk in the northern parts of their range, while cattle are main menu items in Brazil's extensive ranch country, along with caiman and capybaras (large rodents).

- **Example of guild:** South American large predators include 11 members of family Canidae, 1 bear species, 8 relatives of the raccoon, 7 weasel species, 3 kinds of skunk, and 9 other cats besides the jaguar. The largest of those other cats -- pumas and ocelots -- somehow coexist with jaguars throughout their shared range. (*de Oliveira and Pereira; Scognamillo et al.; Smith et al.*)

Red-list status:

Near Threatened. Some local populations are at more risk than others -- check out the latest assessment from the IUCN at https://www.iucnredlist.org/species/15953/123791436 , and the Cat Specialist Group's jaguar page at http://www.catsg.org/index.php?id=95 for more details.

A capybara in the Pantanal, running for its life.
(Image: Jurgens Potgieter/Shutterstock)

Snow leopards

Eric Kilby, https://www.flickr.com/photos/ekilby/44091744752 CC BY-ND 2.0

Name: It's a spotted cat living at high altitudes -- of ***course*** it's called a "snow leopard" (though molecular studies suggest it has a closer evolutionary connection to tigers than to true leopards).

Up through the end of the 20th century and beyond, some experts, like Heptner and Sludskii, also called it an "ounce."

That's not just a measure of weight. It comes from the Old French word *once* that used to be a common name for several spotted wild felines.

You hardly ever see snow leopards called "ounce" any more, but their scientific name preserves this term in Latin: *Panthera uncia*.

Lineage: Panthera.

Outstanding Features:

1. **The longest, densest fur of any big cat** -- up to 5 inches long in wintertime, with some 4,000 guard hairs per square centimeter. (*Cat Specialist Group; Kitchener et al., 2010; Heptner and Sludskii*)

2. That fur hides the fact that **snow leopards are built rather like cheetahs**, with long legs and tail, as well as a very rounded skull. It's all about lifestyle. Cheetahs need speed and balance on the plains. Snow leopards use *their* long legs and tail during intense chases (like this one: https://youtu.be/Uj0EVT-Ekog) over almost vertical terrain. Both cheetah and snow leopard have evolved a rounded skull that widens air passages for them to catch their breath more quickly and to cool down faster after the hunt (in addition, snow leopards need to breathe more often because they live at high altitude, where the air is thinner).

3. **The only cat known to have genetic adaptations similar to those found in people who live at high altitude** (namely, per Wang *et al.*, unique amino acid changes related to factors that increase the number of red blood cells as well as the amount of oxygen-carrying hemoglobin in the blood).

Data: These are from the Cat Specialist Group unless otherwise noted.

- **Weight**: 66 to 110 pounds.

- **Height at the shoulder**: 24 inches. (*Jackson et al.*)

- **Body length**: 35 to 47 inches.

- **Tail length**: 32 to 39 inches. A snow leopard's tail is as thick as a human arm. Besides balancing the cat as it moves, this tail probably also makes a nice warm wrap-around during rest.

- **Coat**: The background color of this very shaggy fur is off white to pale gray. It is covered with rosettes; in addition, there are black spots over the head, neck, and legs. Snow leopards have individualized marking patterns. Two dark lines also typically extend from the neck to the tail. The overall coloration and patterns make snow leopards almost impossible to see against a rocky or snow-covered background. (*Cat*

Eric Kilby,
https://www.flickr.com/photos/ekilby/133602
04225 CC BY-SA 2.0

Specialist Group; Heptner and Sludskii; Jackson et al.; Sunquist and Sunquist; Turner and Antón)

- **Vocals**: Snow leopards lack the right vocal fold qualities to either roar or purr. This doesn't stop them from making other common feline sounds. They also produce a loud yowl during mating season that can be heard above the noise of a fast-moving mountain river and over long distances. And they chuff, as this video shows https://www.youtube.com/watch?v=0cCDqbiGvoQ . (*Cat Specialist Group; Christiansen; Kitchener et al., 2010; Sunquist and Sunquist*)

- **Average litter size**: 1-5; typically 2, per Ewer.

Where found in the wild:

Most snow leopards live in China. They're also found in:

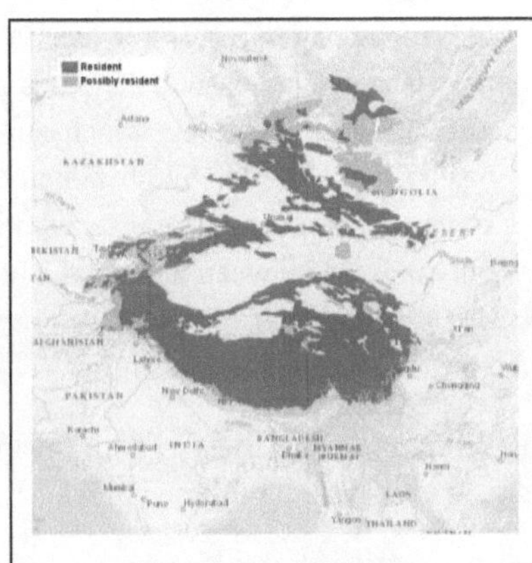

BhagyaMani via Wikimedia, https://commons.wikimedia.org/wiki/File:Sno wLeopard_distribution.jpg CC BY-SA 4.0

- Russia's Altai Mountains. Here, at the northern limit of their range, the cats generally stay below 10,000 feet, sometimes as low as 1600 feet.

- Tian Shan and Kun Lun ranges

- Central Asia's Pamir Mountains

- The Hindu Kush

- The Karakorum Mountains bordering India, Pakistan, Afghanistan, and China

- The Himalayas

Habitat:

- **Range of environments:** Snow leopards have been observed as high as 18,000 feet in the Himalayas, but the Cat Specialist Group notes that they are most often seen between about 9800 to 16,400 feet. These mountain specialists move above and below timberline seasonally with their prey; the lowest reported sighting of a snow leopard is a little under 1,000 feet in the Altai Mountains. (*McCarthy et al.*)

- **Prey base:** Mainly medium-sized hoofed animals, though snow leopards are opportunistic and take marmots and other small prey that they come across. Blue sheep and Siberian ibexes are at the top of the menu -- one snow leopard can take 20 to 30 each year. (*Macdonald et al., 2010*) When wild prey isn't available, snow leopards go after domestic livestock, which can be a heavy blow -- $50 to $300 annually, in some places -- for pastoralists who are only making between $250 and $400

Eric Kilby,
https://www.flickr.com/photos/ekilby/277907
29228 CC BY-SA 2.0

per year. (*Jackson et al.*) As this video at https://youtube.com/watch?v=VNTbzuoivjc shows, ecotourism based on snow leopards can help ease this human-cat conflict.

- **Example of guild:** On the Taxkorgan Nature Reserve, in Central Asia's Pamir mountain range, snow leopards, gray wolves, and the red fox are the main land-based predators. (*Wang et al.*)

Red-list status:

Vulnerable. See the Cat Specialist Group snow leopard page at http://www.catsg.org/index.php?id=100 and the IUCN assessment at https://www.iucnredlist.org/species/22732/50664030 for details.

Clouded leopards

Name: Those beautiful coat markings are the "clouds."

For a long time, no one could be sure about the "leopard" part -- these medium-sized cats combine features of both big cats and their smaller relatives. Given this uncertainty, clouded leopards were put into a special taxonomic category: Neofelis.

Recent genetic testing has confirmed that clouded leopards are indeed big cats. However, they're so different from other members of Panthera that clouded leopards still have their own group.

Their scientific name, as described in international treaties that protect endangered animals, is *Neofelis nebulosa*.

This may change in the future, since phylogenists like Kitchener *et al*. (2017) believe there are two species:

1. *Neofelis nebulosa*: Mainland clouded leopards.

2. *Neofelis diardi*: Sunda clouded leopards (formerly considered a subspecies).

Lineage: Panthera.

Outstanding Features:

1. According to molecular studies, **the oldest line of descent in modern cats**, going back at least five million years and probably more than that. (*Christiansen, 2008a; Kitchener et al., 2017; Werdelin et al.*)

Their greater age may explain why clouded leopards look a little more primitive than other big cats. (Image: surassawadee/Shutterstock)

2. While clouded leopards are **the only big cat with a clouded coat**, a much smaller Southeast Asian feline, the marbled cat, has one, too. Werdelin *et al*. note that marbled cats and clouded leopards are each the oldest group in their respective lineages. These experts raise an interesting question -- could all early cats have had this coat pattern?

Francisco Herrera/Shutterstock

3. **The longest fangs of any cat, in proportion to body size**. Yes, tigers have the longest fangs overall, but they're also very large cats. Canines almost 2 inches long are very unusual on the much smaller clouded leopard! They're not true saberteeth, but no one knows yet why these evolved.

4. **The only big cat capable of rotating its ankles 180 degrees and coming head first out of a tree**. A couple of the smaller cats -- margays and marbled cats -- can do this, too. It's not a primitive throwback, though. Werdelin *et al*. note that the fossils from the first cats show the same kind of feline ankle seen on most of today's cats.

Data: These are from the Cat Specialist Group unless otherwise noted (two values are given since the Group subscribes to the view that there are two clouded leopard species).

- **Weight**: Mainland: 35 to 51 pounds. Sunda: 24 to 55 pounds.

- **Height at the shoulder**: Mainland: 20 to 22 inches. (*Wikipedia; not given on Sunda clouded leopard*)

- **Body length**: 27 to 43 inches (both).

- **Tail length**: 24 to 36 inches (both).

- **Coat**: Dark clouds, stripes, and spots on a background ranging from yellowish-brown to dark gray. Individual clouded leopards can be identified by their coat patterns (*Allen et al.*). Per the Cat Specialist Group, Sunda clouded leopards have smaller "clouds" and a grayer background than their mainland relatives. Sunquist and Sunquist note that all-black (melanistic) clouded leopards are extremely rare but have been reported from Borneo.

- **Vocals**: This big cat purrs! Clouded leopards also make most of the same sounds that small cats do, but do respond to big-cat style chuffing, as shown in this video: https://youtube.com/watch?v=IubJ3rd84ws . They also have a drawn-out moaning call that can be heard at some distance. (*Sunquist and Sunquist*)

- **Average litter size**: 1 to 2 cubs (both). But Ewer notes that this can range from 1 to 4 cubs and is typically, 2 cubs per litter.

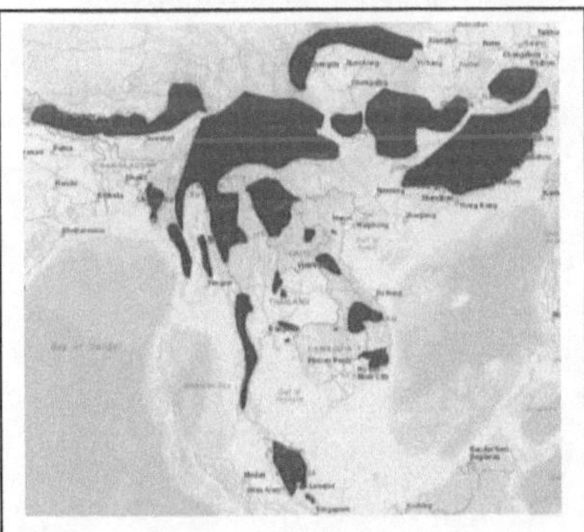

*BhagyaMani via Wikimedia,
https://commons.wikimedia.org/wiki/File:Clou
ded-leopard_distribution.jpg#mw-jump-to-
license CC BY-SA 4.0*

Where found in the wild:

Clouded leopards have been observed from the Himalayan foothills in Nepal (up to 8,000 feet or more) through mainland Southeast Asia into China and southward into peninsular Malaysia, Sumatra, and Borneo.

Their distribution isn't very well understood, since they avoid people and live in the densest part of a forest -- usually, but not always, that's a tropical rainforest.

Habitat: At the time of writing, this isn't very well understood. Check out the references given for this chapter at the end of the book for various studies that discuss a particular clouded leopard habitat, hunting habits, and prey. The big picture still needs to be constructed by a variety of specialists and conservationists.

Red-list status: The IUCN lists both mainland, at

https://www.iucnredlist.org/species/14519/97215090 , and Sunda clouded leopards, at https://www.iucnredlist.org/species/136603/97212874 , as **vulnerable**, for detailed reasons given at those links.

The Cat Specialist Group clouded leopard pages are at http://www.catsg.org/index.php?id=116 for mainland and at http://www.catsg.org/index.php?id=225 for Sunda clouded leopards.

The puma lineage

Pumas

Tambako the Jaguar, https://www.flickr.com/photos/tambako/3820520981 CC BY-ND 2.0

Name: This cat's looks and its tawny coat convinced early Europeans who were exploring the Americas that they had just discovered a new kind of lion.

They hadn't.

We now know that pumas sit on another branch of the cat family tree, one that spans the Old World and the New.

"Puma" comes from a native word. So does "cougar." But the "lion" moniker -- "león" or "leão" in Latin America -- keeps popping up, too.

Among the puma's many other names are:

- Panther

- Painter

- Catamount

- Mountain Cat

- Red tiger

- Screamer (Here's why: https://youtube.com/watch?v=pxo8X5uIWRE)

Scientists call it *Puma concolor*.

Genetic studies confirm that this isn't one of the big cats, despite its lion-like appearance, but the tests aren't as helpful with subspecies. (*Matte et al.*) Up to 32 have been proposed down through the years, but a consensus on puma subgroups is not yet within reach.

Lineage: Puma.

Outstanding Features:

Even a playful youngster like this one has powerful muscles on those hind legs! (Image: Dagmara Ksandrova/Shutterstock)

1. **Fourth largest cat in the world**, after tigers, lions, and jaguars, and **second largest native New World cat.**

2. **The longest hind legs, proportionately, of any member of the cat family**. Combined with a very long and flexible spine, this makes pumas incredibly good at jumping as well as very fast in short chases. But even with a top speed of 40 to 50 mph, pumas can't outsprint their close relative -- the cheetah.

3. **Largest geographic range of any native Western land mammal.** Puma country extends across 110 degrees of latitude, from the tip of South America up into British Columbia's mountains and the Yukon! North American pumas are fairly well known, but since they keep a low profile, particularly in the Amazon Basin, pumas haven't been thoroughly studied yet in Latin America.

Data: This information is from the Cat Specialist Group, except where noted.

- **Weight**: From 110 to about 150 pounds at the Equator to twice that in the extremes of the cat's range north (the Yukon) and south (Patagonia). (*Culver et al.*) Some researchers suggest that size reduction might be one of the ways pumas have evolved to coexist with jaguars in the tropics.

- **Body length**: 3 to 5 feet.

- **Tail length**: 2 to 3 feet.

Tambako the Jaguar,
https://www.flickr.com/photos/tambako/46432
222311 CC BY-ND 2.0

- **Coat**: Newborns often have stripes or spots, but with age, these markings fade into a plain tawny, reddish, silvery-gray, or dark brown coat. Dark brown or black fur dramatically frames the white fur around a puma's mouth. The cat's throat and underparts are white. The tip of its tail is usually black, and so are the backs of its ears. Melanistic (all-black) pumas have been reported. (*Cat Specialist Group; Eizirik et al.*)

- **Vocals:** Although known for their screaming, pumas often sound like domestic cats. They also have a distinctive chirp that sounds like this: https://youtube.com/watch?v=-3UMXnXp-zY

- **Litter size**: 1 to 5 kittens, usually 2 to 3.

Where found in the wild:

These beautiful cats once inhabited North and South America from coast to coast.

Over the last 200 years, they were eradicated in eastern and central North America, except for a small population in Florida. In Latin America, pumas may have lost some 40% of their range because of human activities. (*Caragiulo et al.*)

The good news is that pumas might be returning to eastern North America. They are showing up in parts of the US and Canada east of the Rockies now that their numbers have stabilized in the West, thanks to protective laws and regulated hunting. (*LaRue and Nielsen*)

Believe it or not, this isn't the first time pumas have made a comeback.

Several genetic studies suggest that North American pumas went extinct at the end of the last ice age, along with almost all of the large predators and herbivores that roamed the continent back then. Then, pumas from South America apparently moved north, recolonizing North America! (*Caragiulo et al.; Culver et al.; Matte et al.*)

Habitat:

- **Range of environments:** Adaptability has helped pumas spread across two continents. Today they are found in every major type of habitat except densely populated coastal areas (though pumas can handle some human development). They prefer complex landscapes that have little human presence and offer a mix of forest, understory, uneven ground, and exposed rocks, but pumas are also seen in open spaces with little cover, like the Patagonian grasslands. The only known breeding population in eastern North America, in Florida, inhabits cypress swamps. At the other end of the scale, some sources note that pumas have been seen as high as 19,000 feet in the Andes!

Joshua Tree National Park Flickr account, https://www.flickr.com/photos/joshuatreenp/14 045562840 Public domain

- **Prey base:** In North America, pumas most often go for elk and other hoofed animals. When those are in short supply, they'll hunt smaller prey like raccoons and armadillos, especially in Florida. In Latin America, the puma may select small- to medium-sized animals more often when there are jaguars around. In Chile (where there are no jaguars), larger plant eaters, like the guanaco, are an important part of a puma's diet; in this video, a young puma stalks and kills what might be her first guanaco: https://youtube.com/watch?v=cR6yYpr3gt4 . Livestock predation is a problem in some areas, and in North America, there are 4 to 6 reported puma attacks on people each year. (*Mattson et al.*) The people who made this video -- https://youtu.be/xNJxDWX-qes -- were smart: they weren't hiking alone; they didn't panic; and they kept facing the cat as they slowly backed away.

- **Example of guild:** Pumas live in Yellowstone today with Canada lynxes, bobcats, wolves, coyotes, red foxes, wolverines, badgers, black bears, and grizzly bears. In South America, there is a little more feline competition at the top of the food chain -- jaguars and ocelots. Pumas here have been observed killing smaller predators (and occasionally being murdered by jaguars). Such intraguild killing probably happens in North America, too.

Red-list status:

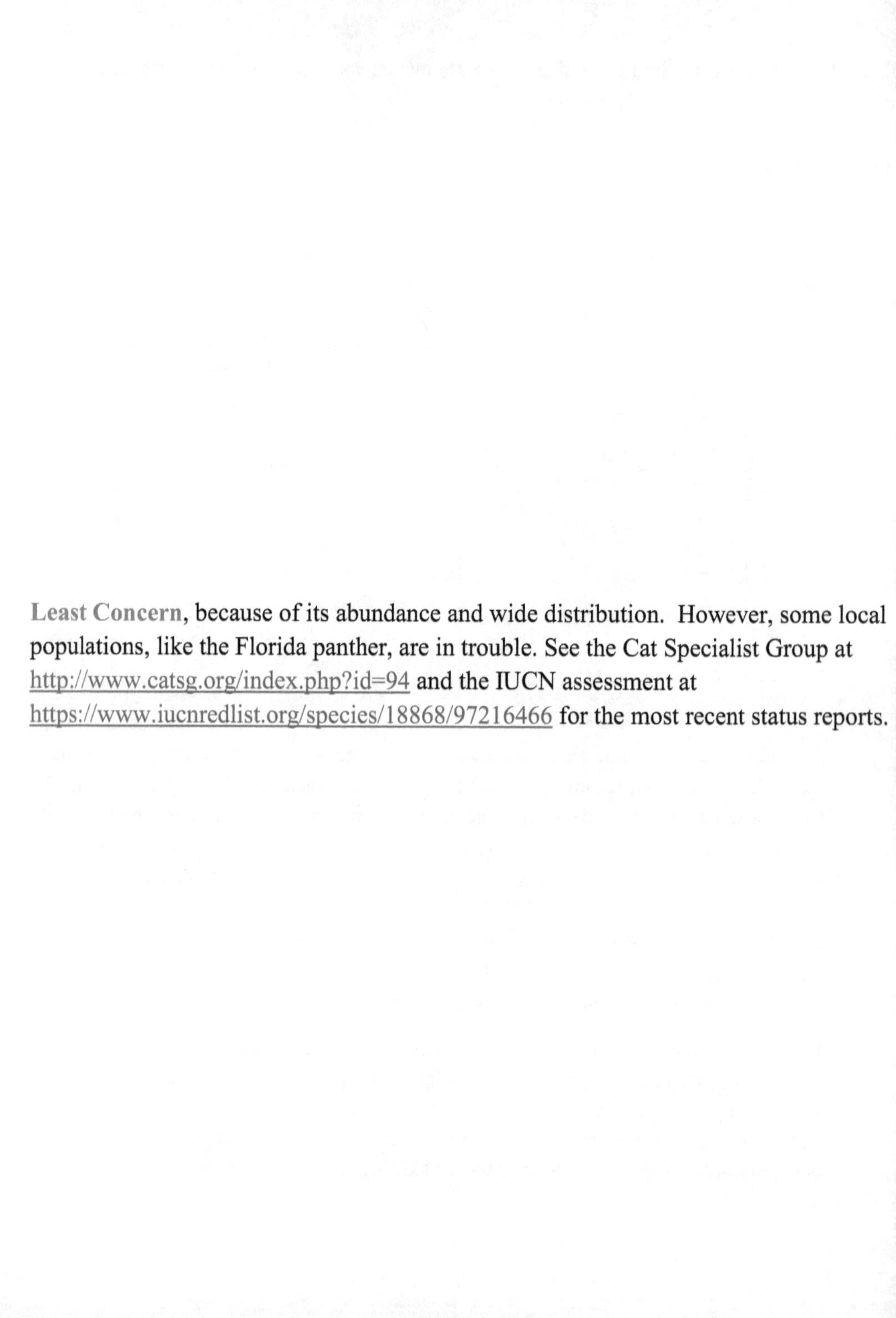

Least Concern, because of its abundance and wide distribution. However, some local populations, like the Florida panther, are in trouble. See the Cat Specialist Group at http://www.catsg.org/index.php?id=94 and the IUCN assessment at https://www.iucnredlist.org/species/18868/97216466 for the most recent status reports.

Jaguarundis

Jaguarundi cubs by Marie Hale, https://www.flickr.com/photos/15016964@N02/6114173142 CC BY 2.0

Name: This widespread Latin American cat has several names, some referring to its variable coat color -- "brown cat," for example, or "Moorish cat" (*gato-mourisco*, in Brazil) -- others, including "otter cat" and "weasel cat," describing the jaguarundi's unusual shape.

For a long time, "jaguarundi" (derived from a native word) was only applied to gray cats, while those with reddish fur were considered a separate species: the "eyra."

Thanks to more research, including camera-trap videos like this -- https://youtube.com/watch?v=fsVwWih7fhs -- we now know that this is all one species, regardless of coat color.

However, giving jaguarundis a formal name is more of a challenge. (See Kitchener *et al.*, page 8, for details.)

Fortunately, we don't have to worry about it in this book. It's enough to simply note that the boffins may call this either *Herpailurus yagouaroundi* or *Puma yagouaroundi*.

Lineage: Puma.

Outstanding Features:

Tambako the Jaguar,
https://www.flickr.com/photos/tambako/10568
663315 , CC BY-ND 2.0

1. At first glance, **this does not really look like a cat**. The head is peculiar. That long body and those short legs are very otter-like. But genetic testing confirms the jaguarundi's membership in family Felidae. It certainly behaves like a cat, too. The other two members of this lineage -- pumas and cheetahs -- also have long flexible bodies and small heads, though they have retained a more feline appearance. We may never learn how or why the jaguarundi went down its particular evolutionary path.

2. **One of the few cats that commonly comes in more than one color**. (*Ewer*) Feline coat colors do vary -- leopards, for instance, are very pale in the Russian Far East but intensely colored near the Equator. However, few cat species regularly show completely different colors. Giordano identifies three typical jaguarundi coats: dark brown/gray (most common); red to yellowish-red (second most common); and grayish silver. All colors can show up in a single litter.

3. **Jaguarundis have at least 13 different calls**. These range from purrs to whistles and chattering up to chirping like a bird. (*Cat Specialist Group*) Most cats aren't that vocal. Unfortunately, multiple YouTube searches only show these cats making more typical feline sounds like hisses or calls to their young, like this: https://youtu.be/pi94gxt5pvQ

Data: Per the Cat Specialist Group (except as noted):

- **Weight**: 7 to 15 pounds.

- **Height at the shoulder**: 1 to 2 feet (*Johnson*)

- **Body length**: 19 to 31 inches.

- **Tail length**: 11 to 23 inches.

- **Coat**: Kittens often have light spots, which fade as they mature. (*Johnson*) The adult coat is plain red, dark brown/gray, or silvery, with somewhat lighter coloration on the head and perhaps a few faint marks here and there, usually on the legs.

- **Litter size**: 1 to 4 cubs.

A "Moorish (dark gray) cat" in the Sao Paulo Zoo. (Image: Fabio Manfredini,"https://www.flickr.com/photos/fab iomanfredini/6067174380 CC BY 2.0)

Where found in the wild:

This jaguarundi is in an Ecuadorian rescue center. (Image: Carine06, https://www.flickr.com/photos/435 55660@N00/16071816328 CC BY-SA 2.0)

Jaguarundis are small, shy, and very difficult to catch for radiotelemetry studies. As a result, their distribution and life in the wild aren't very well known.

While not as widespread as pumas, jaguarundis do range across almost 60 degrees of latitude, from central Argentina up through South America and Central America into northern Mexico.

It's not clear whether there are any left in the US. The last one confirmed was seen in 1986, per Caso.

Nevertheless, a few sightings are still reported in southern Texas and Arizona, as well as in Florida and coastal Alabama.

Habitat:

- **Range of environments:** Jaguarundis apparently prefer lowlands, but they've been seen up to 10,000 feet in Colombia. Most habitats will do, as long as there is plenty of cover, although jaguarundis are most common in open areas like thorn scrub, gallery forests along riverbeds, and in mixed grassland/woods. While they avoid people, jaguarundis do live in farmlands and other human-altered environments.

- **Prey base:** Usually mammals, birds, and reptiles weighing 2 pounds or less. Predation on poultry and other small domestic livestock is a problem in some areas, too. Sometimes the cat will go after a larger animal. In this video, the jaguarundi goes after a monkey -- it's a ghastly struggle for them both (note that jaguarundis are reportedly ground hunters, yet this one easily follows its hapless victim through the tree tops): https://youtube.com/watch?v=o6HIDSwwhek .

- **Example of guild:** Jaguarundis are never the dominant cat species in an ecosystem. (*Caso et al.*) Jaguars, pumas, and/or ocelots are typically present, as well as a few cats closer in size to the jaguarundi -- margays, pampas cats, tiger cats, Geoffroy cats, or even bobcats, depending on location. As we will see in the book on South American cats, smaller cats avoid ocelots; this "ocelot effect" (*de Oliveira et al.*) limits jaguarundi numbers in some areas.

Red-list status:

Overall, Least Concern, although jaguarundis in various local regions are at higher risk, per the IUCN at https://www.iucnredlist.org/species/9948/50653167 and the Cat Specialist Group's jaguarundi page at http://www.catsg.org/index.php?id=93 .

Cheetahs

Name: "Cheetah" comes from the Hindu word *chetah* -- "spotted one." (*Cat Specialist Group*)

The scientific name is *Acinonyx jubatus*. Translated from Latin, that means "non-moving claws" and "maned" or "crested." (This will make more sense when we get to the cheetah's unique features.)

Genetic testing shows some differences among various cheetah populations but study results aren't clear enough yet to establish beyond any doubt which of these groups, if any, are true cheetah subspecies. (*Cat Specialist Group*)

Lineage: Puma. That's right -- molecular research proves that cheetahs aren't one of the big cats. (*Johnson et al.; Nyakatura and Bininda-Emonds*)

Outstanding Features:

1. **World's fastest land mammal**. (*Cat Specialist Group*) No surprise here. Authorities differ on what the cheetah's top speed might be. The 100-mph claims you might see online aren't true. But, with documented records of 58 to 64-plus mph, cheetahs will always leave greyhounds (top speed 38 mph) in the dust (by the way, per Snopes at https://www.snopes.com/fact-check/cheetah-greyhound-audi-ad/ , the famous photo of a cheetah at the dog races was faked; however, someone *did* set up a real-life greyhound/cheetah race in 1937, which the cat won). Cheetahs can also accelerate faster than other cats, taking just 2 seconds to go from a standing start to 50 mph. (*Cat Specialist Group; Hudson et al.; Krausman and Morales; Wikipedia*)

Charles Barilleaux,
https://www.flickr.com/photos/bontempscharly
/4939723799, CC BY 2.0

2. Not coincidentally, cheetahs have the **most specialized body of any cat today**. (*Kitchener et al., 2010*) How can living tissue do "zero to 50"? To find out, National Geographic used ultra-high-speed cameras to film running cheetahs in 2012. Here's one of the resulting slow-motion videos, with a spit-second timer on the left counting elapsed time: https://youtube.com/watch?v=_oEA18Y8gM0 Look how much action the cheetah packs into just 2 seconds. It took a lot of evolution for life to develop such a running machine! The anatomical details are very technical, of course (for example, this: https://youtube.com/watch?v=icFMTB0Pi0g). Let's just look at an adaptation that inspired the name *Acinonyx* - "non-moving claws." Cheetahs have typical feline claws but, *except for the dewclaw*, they lack most of the protective surrounding paw tissue that serves as a sheath. Those claws therefore stick out and soon become blunt. That's nice for cheetahs, who now have 4 "running spikes" on each foot (*Macdonald et al., 2010*) to boost their speed. On digit 5, which never touches the ground, *the dewclaw does have a sheath and is very sharp*. Why? Because, at the "finish line," cheetahs don't have sufficient energy left to wrestle prey to the ground for a killing bite. Instead, they reach out and snag their running meal with a dewclaw to bring it down.

Maggie Meyer/Shutterstock

3. **Cheetah cubs look weird**. During their

first 3 months, baby cheetahs sport Mohawks, that is, a mantle of long grayish blue hair running from each cub's forehead to the tip of its tail. These long hairs fall out over time, though adolescents and young adults sometimes keep a short mane. Mantles are the reason for the scientific name *jubatus* -- "maned" or "crested." Since they give cheetah cubs a honey-badger look (this is one of the local small predators, and feisty for its size), some researchers suggest mantles evolved as mimicry to scare predators off. But a more common explanation is that mantles help cubs blend into the background while Mom is away hunting. Each day cheetah cubs must be left alone for hours in open terrain. There are many land and air predators in cheetah country and up to two-thirds of the cubs die before they are 3 months old. That sad statistic is even worse if there are lions around – they seem to take cheetahs personally and will kill them on sight. There isn't much a mother cheetah can do when she comes home to a tragedy like this. Perhaps the mantles are why two-thirds of the litter in this video survived a lion attack: https://youtube.com/watch?v=ec2JfHharlo . (*Cat Specialist Group; Durant; Heptner and Sludskii; Kelly*)

4. **Cheetahs have had their genetic reset button pressed at least twice in the last 100,000 years**. The last time it happened was about 10,000 years ago, at the end of the last ice age. (As red-listed cats, cheetahs are also in a bottleneck now, but that is too recent to show up yet in the genome.) Fossils don't clearly record what happened. Perhaps cheetahs had a close brush with extinction, especially during the crisis 10,000 years ago, when supersized land mammals died out almost everywhere except Africa. However, the cause might also have been factors that haven't left fossils behind, like population dynamics. Whatever the reason(s) behind them, these resets have left today's cheetahs with very little genetic variability, putting these lovely cats at even more risk of extinction. (*Cat Specialist Group; Charruau et al.; Dobrynin et al.; Faurby et al.; Krausman and Morales; Macdonald et al, 2010; O'Brien et al., 2017; Werdelin et al.*)

5. **A unique social organization**. (*Cat Specialist Group*) Most cats that aren't lions lead solitary lives. Cheetahs, on the other hand, are surprisingly social. Upon reaching independence at around age 18 months, siblings often live together as a group for about 6 months -- after all, just because they don't need Mom any more doesn't mean that they are now masters of the high-speed hunt. If they hang together during this make-or-break part of the learning curve, their chances for survival are improved. Females will eventually

A male coalition in the Maasai Mara. (Image: Ray in Manila, https://www.flickr.com/photos/rayinmanila/43 941746162 CC BY 2.0)

drop out of the group when it's time for their first litter. However, males (related or unrelated) may form a coalition for life. (*Cat Specialist Group; Durant; Krausman and Morales; Macdonald et al., 2010a*)

Data: This information is from the Cat Specialist Group, except where noted.

- **Weight**: 77 to 143 pounds. The smallest cheetahs live in deserts and other very dry lands.

- **Height at the shoulder**: 28 to 35 inches. (*Wikipedia*)

- **Body length**: 45 to 55 inches.

- **Tail length**: 24 to 33 inches.

- **Coat**: Tawny, pale yellow, or grayish background fur, covered with lots of small dark spots but no rosettes. Per Ewer, someone once counted 1,967 spots on a cheetah! Sometimes, especially in southern Africa, these spots broaden and form short stripes as a result of the "king cheetah" genetic mutation. A cheetah's underparts are generally pale or white. That long tail, so useful in maintaining balance at high speed, has a white tip; its upper surface is spotted; and dark rings encircle the last third of the tail. Cheetahs also have unique facial "tear lines" -- a single dark line extending from the inner corner of each eye down to the outer corner of the cat's mouth. (*Cat Specialist Group; Krausman and Morales*)

The "king cheetah" mutation. (Image: Steve Jurvetson, https://www.flickr.com/photos/jurvetson/50458 75596 CC BY 2.0

- **Vocals:** Cheetahs do not roar or scream. Since they are easily tamed, there are many thoroughly relaxing online videos of them purring. Here is one that also showcases a few of the other sounds this chatty wild cat makes: https://youtu.be/3kFl_TY3iUg

- **Litter size**: 4 to 6 cubs.

Where found in the wild:

Cheetahs used to be widespread from India through southwestern Asia and the Middle East into almost all of Africa's woodland savannahs and arid flat lands.

They have lost about 90% of that historic range, mainly due to loss of prey and habitat, as well as because of the once popular but unsustainable royal custom of capturing cheetahs and training them for hunting.

There aren't a lot of cheetahs out there now -- fewer than 7,000 adults, all told, living in 29 known subpopulations -- but they still have a wide distribution in southern and eastern Africa, with strongholds in Namibia/Botswana and Kenya/Tanzania. There are also an estimated 80 Asiatic cheetahs in Iran's central deserts. (*Cat Specialist Group; Durant et al.*)

Habitat:

- **Range of environments:**   Cheetahs are very well adapted to dry climates but can thrive in any habitat that supports their special lifestyle (this rules out tropical rainforest, swamps, steep slopes, and other landscapes that hinder high-speed chases).

Demetrius John Kessy,
https://www.flickr.com/photos/diamondglacier
adventures/5613298173 CC BY 2.0

- **Prey base:** Medium-sized (about 22- to 125-pound) planet eaters, like impalas, Thomson's gazelles, and warthogs. Coalitions can take larger animals.   Cheetahs will eat smaller mammals and ground birds during hard times, as this video shows (a desert cheetah catching a mouse!): https://youtube.com/watch?v=PGZuE0H82Gg There are no reports of cheetahs attacking people in the wild.

- **Example of guild:** In the Kalahari, a study conducted in Kgalagadi Transfrontier Park found cheetahs, lions, leopards, and hyenas in the large predator guild. Smaller carnivores there included caracals, jackals, foxes, honey badgers, genets, black-footed cats, and African wildcats. (*Herbst*)

Red-list status:

Cheetahs have been listed as Vulnerable since the 1980s.

In addition, three populations are considered critically endangered (*Durant et al.*):
- Iran
- Northwest Africa
- Populations in northern and western Africa

See the Cat Specialist Group's cheetah page at http://www.catsg.org/index.php?id=107 and the IUCN assessment at https://www.iucnredlist.org/species/219/50649567 for more details.

The Lynx Lineage

Upper left, **Canada lynx**: *Keith Williams,* https://flickr.com/photos/46306125@N03/4464643075 *CC BY 2.0; Upper right,* **Eurasian lynx**: *Thomas Gerhard, https://www.flickr.com/photos/thomasgerhard/15127125495 CC BY-ND 2.0; Lower left,* **Bobcat**: *docentjoyce, https://www.flickr.com/photos/docentjoyce/3995884459 CC BY 2.0; Lower right,* **Iberian lynx**: *Agami Photo Agency/Shutterstock*

Bobcats

Name: In some languages, this is called the "red lynx" -- that's why its scientific name is *Lynx rufus*. But early English settlers in North America were more fascinated by that short tail. To them, it was a "bobbed cat."

Another name for bobcats is "wildcat." This may seem a little strange to people from Europe, Asia, or Africa who only know the original wildcat -- *Felis silvestris*.

F. silvestris never made it to the Americas (though a close relative, the domestic cat, traveled there with the first Europeans).

Lynxes did reach North America. And now it's bobcats, not true wildcats, that call to one another here, through echoing forests or, as in this video, across the still desert air: https://youtu.be/ZsFC3GLzw6w

Lineage: Lynx.

Outstanding Features:

1. **How to tell bobcats and Canada lynxes apart**. These two species mingle on either side of the US/Canada border. If you see a lynx-like cat here, **check out its tail**: the tip of a bobcat's tail is black on top and white underneath; the Canada lynx has a completely black tail tip. If you're lucky enough to get a really close view, are **the paws** unusually large? Then that's probably the Canada lynx, which has evolved a sort of "snowshoe"; bobcat paws are more proportional (which means these

Bobcat, left, by Becky Matsubara, https://www.flickr.com/photos/beckymatsubara /48684991041 CC BY 2.0; Canada lynx (right), by Eric Kilby, https://www.flickr.com/photos/ekilby/1271145 5063 CC BY-SA 2.0

cats can't handle deep snow as well as Canada lynxes do). Bobcats also have a shorter beard and ear tufts, as well as a somewhat smaller head.

Bobcat in a New Mexican cottonwood tree. (Image: National Park Service, https://www.flickr.com/ph otos/iip-photo- archive/36900726792 public domain)

2. **The most common North American wild cat**. Not even pumas outnumber bobcats here. That's a surprise, since pumas range over far more ground -- from the tip of South America up into the Yukon. My guess is that this is because the bobcat has larger litters and is better able to tolerate people -- for instance, you won't see pumas relaxing by a swimming pool like this: https://youtube.com/watch?v=NcceSCuMtG0

3. **The oldest lynx species**. Lynx evolution has confounded paleontologists down through the years. Today's genetic testing helps clear up some of the mystery. Molecular markers suggest that lynxes last shared a common ancestor with other lineages -- puma and Felis -- back in the Miocene, some 7 to 12 million years ago. Then ancestral lynxes took off on their own evolutionary path, eventually producing the bobcat about 3.5 million to 5 million years ago, during the Pliocene epoch. The other three lynx species showed up a little later, in early Pleistocene times. (*Gradstein et al.; Johnson and others [younger dates]; Nyakatura and Bininda- Emonds [older dates]; Werdelin et al.*)

4. **Hybridizes with the Canada lynx**. Bobcats and Canada lynxes have one of the world's best documented hybrid zones, extending along both sides of the US/Canada border. DNA studies indicate that this interbreeding probably has been going on a long time, though it's not widespread enough to threaten either species with something called "cryptic extinction" -- where an animal looks the same on the outside but has lost its original genetic heritage through interbreeding with other species. (*Kelly et al.; Li et al.; Macdonald et al., 2010a*)

Data: This information is from the Cat Specialist Group, except where noted. Bobcat size varies quite a bit across its wide range, with the largest animals most commonly seen in the north.

- **Weight**: 13 to 44 pounds
- **Height at the shoulder**: 12 to 24 inches. (*Wikipedia*)
- **Body length**: 20 to 47 inches.
- **Tail length**: 4 to 10 inches.
- **Coat**: The thick, soft fur comes in more colors than red, including tan, brown, yellowish brown, tawny, and pale gray -- it all depends on where the individual lives. Coat patterns vary, too. Some bobcats are unmarked, while others have brown or black spots and/or stripes. All bobcats have light-colored fur on the underparts, sometimes with dark marks. A few black (melanistic) bobcats, and some albinos, have been seen, too. Like all lynxes, bobcats have black ear tufts, but these and the famous lynx "beard" aren't as fully

Linda Tanner,
https://www.flickr.com/photos/goingslo/54880 97878 CC BY 2.0

developed. Bobcats often curl their tails, displaying the white side prominently, likely as a visual signal to other bobcats. (*Cat Specialist Group; Ewer*)

- **Litter size**: 1 to 8. In addition, Ewer notes that bobcats may sometimes have two litters per year.

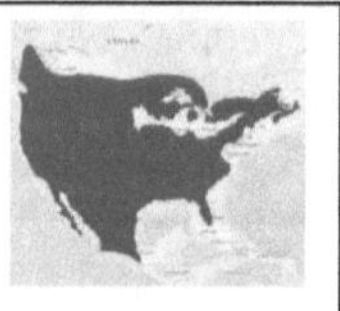

Bobcat range today. (Image: BhagyaMani via Wikimedia https://commons.w ikimedia.org/wiki/F ile:Bobcat_distribut ion2016.jpg#mw-jump-to-license , CC BY-SA 4.0)

Where found in the wild:

Bobcats are widespread, but during most of the 20th century, they disappeared from much of the midwestern US.

In the 1990s, conservation measures, reintroductions, and the bobcat's own resilience brought these lynxes back to every Lower 48 US state except, for some reason, Delaware.

Winter snow depth probably limits their range in the north - bobcats can't handle deep snow like the Canada lynx can.

Far to the south, in Mexico's Oaxaca State, competition from the margay, ocelot, jaguarundi, and jaguar probably keeps bobcats from spreading any farther down into Central America.

Habitat:

- **Range of environments:**   Bobcats have been seen from sea level up to more than 11,000 feet on Mexican volcanoes. They seem to prefer low to middle elevations, and woodlands rather than open areas. However, as long as prey is abundant and there's enough cover for hunting and raising families, the bobcat is comfortable almost everywhere -- from northern conifer stands, through bottomland hardwoods and coastal swamps in the South, to the Southwest's arid grasslands and thorn scrub. In Mexico, bobcats also prowl through tropical dry forests of pine, oak, and fir trees. They live in some urban areas, too, like Tucson, Arizona -- there doesn't seem to be much resulting conflict, just many online videos of a beautiful but wary lynx, quietly hanging out in the back yard or on the porch.

Larry Zuckerman/BLM Wyoming,
https://www.flickr.com/photos/134389515@N0
6/29343617684 CC BY 2.0

- **Prey base**: Bobcats share the Canada lynx's taste for rabbit and hare. They're not as dependent on this prey as their northern cousin is, though, and will also take a variety of small mammals and birds -- whatever's most abundant in their area. Occasionally a bobcat may even crave seafood, as this video shows: https://youtube.com/watch?v=jo_zCB7AcKo
- **Example of guild**: In Pleistocene times, bobcats in what is now Yellowstone Park had to deal with dire wolves and sabercats, in addition to modern coyotes, pumas, wolves, and bears. (*Van Valkenburgh*) Nowadays, other predators that bobcats may encounter across their wide range include coyotes, foxes, pumas, raccoons, skunks, and even domestic dogs and cats. Don't feel too sorry for them. In the north, bobcats are both aggressive and large enough to take territory from the Canada lynx. In southern Texas and northwestern Mexico, they can outcompete ocelots in conifer woods or dry habitats. Farther south, though, in the tropical forests, margays and jaguarundis, as well as ocelots, probably have the edge. (*Sanchez-Cordero et al.; Major and Sherburne; McCord*)

Red-list status:

Least concern. That's despite bobcats being the most heavily harvested cat species in the fur trade. This practice appears to be sustainable, but there are issues. For more details, see the Cat

Specialist Group's bobcat page at http://www.catsg.org/index.php?id=96 and the IUCN's latest assessment at https://www.iucnredlist.org/species/12521/50655874 .

Canada lynxes

Name: Even its scientific name -- *Lynx canadensis* -- tells you where this famous cat lives. However, Canada lynxes are common in Alaska, too, and a few even inhabit the Lower 48.

The word "lynx" comes from an Old French name for many kinds of spotted cat: *l'once* -- the ounce. (Yes, that's an old-timey name for snow leopards, too.)

People mistakenly kept *le* ("the") when they adopted this term into their own language for cats now known in English and French as lynx, *lince* in Spanish and Italian.

Lineage: Lynx.

Outstanding Features:

1. **Canada's most widespread wild cat**. This lynx species still covers about 95% of its historic range. However, it is less common now in southern and eastern Canada. (*Poole; Vashon*)

2. **Moves more easily through deep snow than any other carnivore in the region**. This is possible thanks to oversized paws that have lots of dense fur growing in between the toe pads. (*Cat Specialist Group; Kitchener et al., 2010*) These insulated "snowshoes" help the Canada lynx race over and through snow.

It's easier to see the huge paws when there's no snow cover. Krystal Hamlin, https://www.flickr.com/photos/krystalhamlin/2 8825656158 CC BY 2.0

3. **The only cat known to have prey-driven population cycles.** All cats thrive in times of plenty and starve when prey numbers dwindle. However, Canada lynxes have their own take on this natural process. Their numbers rise and fall along with snowshoe hare "boom/bust" cycles that play out over roughly 8 to 11 years. According to one estimate, the total lynx population in Canada might be over 500,000 at peak hare population time, their numbers plummeting to just 50,000 as hares go through a "bust." Then the cycle starts anew and the lynx population starts growing again. This cycle even shows up in Canadian fur trading records going back some 3 centuries! (*Cat Specialist Group; MacDonald et al.; O'Donoghue et al.; Poole*)

4. **Hybridizes with the bobcat**. For many millennia, Canada lynx and bobcats have been mingling their genes wherever they meet along what is now the border between the United States and Canada. Wildlife biologists have discovered several hybrid lynx groups here, but they also note separate populations of "pure" bobcat and Canada lynx. Since this hybridization has been going on for a while, it's likely that the balance between hybrids and "purebreds" will last into the foreseeable future. (*Li et al.; Schwartz et al.*)

Data: This information is from the Cat Specialist Group, except where noted.

- **Weight:** 18 to 27 pounds.

- **Height at the shoulder:** 19 to 22 inches. (*Wikipedia, 2020*)

Eric Kilby, https://www.flickr.com/photos/ekilby/8154273 321 CC BY-SA 2.0

*Jeremiah John McBride,
https://www.flickr.com/photos/bullfrogphoto/3
411472257/in/photostream/ CC BY-ND 2.0*

- **Body length:** 29 to 42 inches.

- **Tail length:** 4 to 6 inches.

- **Coat:** Reddish brown to grayish brown, with hairs tipped in light gray or white. During winter, the coat is much thicker and lighter colored. Fur on the underparts is always pale. All-black lynxes haven't been reported, but there is a "blue lynx," especially in Alaska, that may be a partial albino mutation. Canada lynxes have very faint spots, compared to the dramatic spotting on an Iberian lynx (*Lynx pardinus*). Long fur makes Canada lynxes appear larger than they really are (twice as big as a house cat but only half the weight of a Eurasian lynx). Their tail is ringed, with a black tip, and they have the typical black ear tufts, as well as a ruff of fur all around their face that's especially heavy in wintertime. (*Allen et al.; Cat Specialist Group; Poole*)

- **Vocals**: I did not find much information about lynx communication -- presumably, these cats purr and make other typical small-cat sounds. But during breeding season, male Canada lynxes are incredibly loud, as this video shows: https://youtube.com/watch?v=G4ewNJ77xT8

- **Litter size**: 1 to 8. During the "bust" part of a snowshoe hare cycle, lynxes may not have any kits at all. They'll make up for it in later years when hares are thriving. (*Cat Specialist Group; O'Donoghue et al.; Poole*)

Where found in the wild:

Canada lynxes live wherever there are snowshoe hares.

That means up to tree line in the Arctic. The cat's range has shrunk in southern and eastern Canada, where people have moved in.   These lynxes are now rare in the east and have actually disappeared from Prince Edward Island and mainland Nova Scotia.

Historically, the Canada lynx also roamed across several northern US states, along with bobcats. Today, while common in Alaska, breeding

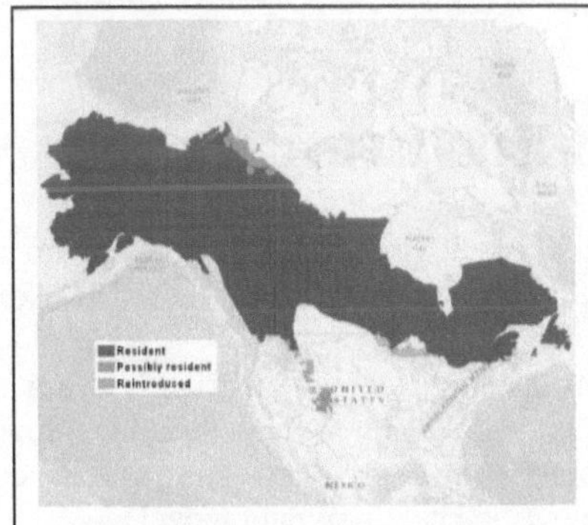

*Canada lynxes have disappeared from some of the eastern parts of their historic range.
(Image: BhagyaMani via Wikimedia
https://commons.wikimedia.org/wiki/File:Can
adaLynx_distribution2016.jpg#mw-jump-to-
license CC BY-SA 4.0)*

populations have been found in only 4 states: Washington, Montana, Minnesota, and Maine.

An attempted reintroduction of the Canada lynx in New York State during the 1980s failed. A new group has been established in the Colorado Rockies, but it's too early to tell if this attempt to bring back the Canada lynx will succeed.

Habitat:

- **Range of environments:**   Canada lynx chase snowshoe hares through taiga and mountain forests of mixed conifers and hardwoods (this link explains what taiga is: https://www.nationalgeographic.org/encyclopedia/taiga/). They will cross meadows and farmlands, and even swim across rivers, but they never linger in such exposed places. Ideal Canada lynx habitat is a forest that burned or otherwise opened up at least 20 years ago and has grown back in with open canopy and the sort of dense understory that hares prefer. Old logging sites also work, but these often lack the downed trees and upturned stumps that Canada lynx typically use to raise a family.(*Cat Specialist Group; O'Donoghue et al.; Poole; Vashon*)

- **Prey base**: Up to 97% of the Canada lynx's diet is snowshoe hare, per the Cat Specialist Group. When bunnies aren't abundant in one place or another, particularly in the southern parts of the range, the cats will either migrate to find more hares or switch over to birds and other small mammals. They occasionally even take down deer, sheep, and caribou calves.

- **Example of guild**: Today, Yellowstone's predator guild includes pumas, Canada lynx, bobcats, wolves, coyotes, red foxes, wolverines, badgers, black bears, and grizzly bears. (*Van Valkenburgh*)

Red-list status:

Least concern. However, Canada lynx are considered "endangered" in New Brunswick and Nova Scotia, and "threatened" in the US (except Alaska).

All lynx species except the Iberian lynx are harvested for their fur. Canada lynx are legally trapped in Alaska and several Canadian provinces without negative effects on their overall numbers. However, this harvesting is reduced or prohibited during the "bust" years of the lynx/snowshoe hare population cycle.

For more information on the Canada lynx's status, check out the Cat Specialist Group's page at http://www.catsg.org/index.php?id=97 and the most recent Red List assessment by the IUCN at https://www.iucnredlist.org/species/12518/101138963 .

.

Eurasian lynxes

Name: It's an appropriate one -- the Eurasian lynx prowls the continent from its Atlantic shores (Scandinavia) to the Pacific (Russian Far East), and southward into Central Asia.

The Eurasian lynx's scientific name -- *Lynx lynx* -- once was applied to a group identified as "northern lynxes." "Southern lynxes," with their more vivid colors and darker spots, were called *Lynx pardina*.

But appearances can be deceiving. Genetic tests and other studies now show there to be two lynx species on the northern continents. Only the one in Eurasia is *Lynx lynx* (the Canada lynx has a different name).

and

in

In some languages, the word "lynx" seems related to various Indo-European words for "light," perhaps because of this cat's beautiful eyes. (Image: Tambako the Jaguar, https://www.flickr.com/photos/tambako/17157 696991 CC BY-ND 2.0)

Too, some former members of *L. pardina*, like Caucasus Mountain lynxes and those in southern Europe (not including the Iberian Peninsula), are actually *L. lynx* despite their brighter, more distinctly spotted coats.

Taxonomists still haven't settled the question of Eurasian lynx subspecies, though.

Lineage: Lynx.

Outstanding Features:

1. **The largest lynx species**.   Eurasian lynxes are twice as heavy as Canada lynxes and up to 4 times the size of a house cat. No wonder that this is the only lynx that routinely takes down plant-eaters like deer and reindeer! Like its close relatives, though, the Eurasian lynx also hunts smaller prey, including hares, rodents, and birds.

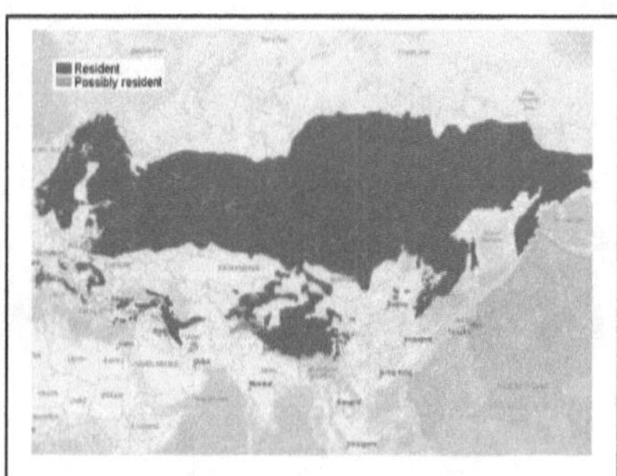

BhagyaMani via https://commons.wikimedia.org/wiki/File:Euro peanLynx_distribution2015.jpg#mw-jump-to-license Wikimedia, CC BY-SA 4.0

2. **One of today's most wide-ranging wild cat species**. Leopards, found from the Russian Far East to the tip of Africa, may have the north-south axis covered, but Eurasian lynx country spans a respectable 3,800 miles from east to west and another 2,000 miles or so down to the Himalayas.

3. **Third largest predator in Europe**. The Eurasian lynx used to be common here, along with wolves and brown bears. All three carnivores are rare these days, even after several successful lynx reintroduction programs, but lynxes do still maintain a European presence. These separate scenes of a wolf and a lynx in the wild were filmed recently in Sweden: https://youtube.com/watch?v=W6AAXPLHC08

Data:

This information is from the Cat Specialist Group, except where noted.

- **Weight**: 38 to 55 pounds.
- **Height at the shoulder**: 26 inches (*Breitenmoser et al., 2000*)
- **Body length**: 35 to 47 inches.
- **Tail length**: 8 to 9 inches.

- **Coat**: Dense and silky fur, with a very thick undercoat in winter. Background color is highly variable -- generally, it is some shade of gray, reddish, or yellow. Eurasian lynxes have three pattern types: spotted, barred, and mostly unspotted (very rare). Their underparts are usually white, and so is the trademark lynx "beard," though this often shows dark patterning with black-tipped hairs. Ear tufts are always black, matching the tip of the bobbed tail. While not as good at snowshoeing as their North American cousins, Eurasian lynx do grow a furry layer that completely covers their paw pads during wintertime. (*Breitenmoser et al., 2000; Cat Specialist Group; Heptner and Sludskii*)
- **Vocals**: I haven't learned whether male Eurasian lynxes screech during breeding season, but check out this video of a lynx family chatting together (and watch, at the end, as a solitary kit suddenly makes what is probably its first kill): https://youtube.com/watch?v=9y2N-p93kF4
- **Litter size**: 1 to 4.

Where found in the wild:

Back in the days when most of Europe was forested, Eurasian lynxes probably were everywhere. They even lived in northern England up to early medieval times. (*Hetherington et al*)

As the human population increased and Europe's forests were cut down, Eurasian lynxes disappeared from all but a few places -- the Carpathian Mountains, southeastern Balkans, Fennoscandia, the Baltic States, and European Russia.

Tambako the Jaguar,
https://www.flickr.com/photos/tambako/14447
577135 CC BY-ND 2.0

They're making a comeback in Europe now, thanks to conservation laws and reintroduction, though such programs are controversial because of possible effects on livestock and game animals.

Farther east, some lynxes are seen in parts of Central Asia and on the Tibetan Plateau, but three-quarters of the Eurasian lynx's range is in Russia, extending from the Urals westward to Kamchatka on the Pacific coast.

Human history has actually helped lynxes here.

Their numbers increased over the 20th century as war, revolution, and collectivization of agriculture during the Soviet Union era reduced hunting pressure on both lynxes and their prey. (*Heptner and Sludskii*)

Habitat:

- **Range of environments**:   Eurasian lynxes are adaptable enough to range from sea level up to alpine meadows above timberline, but they prefer a variety of forest types at more moderate elevations. Their ideal habitat has lots of prey, of course, as well as what Heptner and Sludskii call "fort-like" places -- rocks, talus slopes, tall trees or windfalls (for escape or as den sites) -- and an annual snow cover of less than 20 inches.

"Iz not a fort -- iz a chaise lounge." -- Eurasian lynx. (Image: Travel Stock/Shutterstock)

- **Prey base**: In Europe, it's usually hoofed animals, particularly small deer. In parts of Russia, lynxes hunt arctic hares out on the flat taiga and small hoofed animals in more mountainous regions. During the snow-free months, they also go for rodents and birds occasionally. Breitenmoser *et al.* (2000) note that there is no record of unprovoked attacks on people. However, Eurasian lynxes do have a taste for domestic animals, which leads to conflict with livestock owners and gamekeepers.
- **Example of guild**: Lynxes are part of a northern European predator guild that includes foxes and wolverines, as well as bears and wolves. As another example, in the Russian Far East they must also contend with tigers, badgers, and martens.

Red-list status:

Least concern, given the wide distribution and stability of Eurasian lynx populations in many places.

However, some smaller groups, like the Balkan lynx, are still at high risk of extinction, while many reintroduced lynxes in western and central Europe are struggling to get established. The Cat Specialist Group's Eurasian lynx page at http://www.catsg.org/index.php?id=99 and the IUCN assessment at https://www.iucnredlist.org/species/12519/121707666 have lots of information about this.

Iberian lynxes

Agami Photo Agency/Shutterstock

Name: Back in the day, this medium-sized wild cat -- found only on the Iberian Peninsula, in Spain and Portugal -- used to be filed under "southern lynx" (*Lynx pardina*) along with other lynxes that had colorful coats and dark spots.

As knowledge of the lynx family improved, the Iberian lynx then became known as a Eurasian lynx subspecies. But early in the 21st century, molecular testing confirmed that Iberian lynxes are indeed a unique species.

They alone deserve the scientific name that was once applied to all "southern lynxes." Corrected for modern usage, that's *Lynx pardinus*.

Lineage: Lynx.

Outstanding Features:

1. **Only found on the Iberian Peninsula**. Iberian lynx fossils have been found in France and northern Italy, but that was before the last ice age. As the Arctic ice cap moved south, warmth-loving life had only two choices: go extinct or get out of the way. One refuge for lynxes and other animals and plants was the Iberian Peninsula: that part of mainland Europe now occupied by Spain and Portugal. Then, some 12,000 years ago, as things warmed up, tundra and permafrost that had once extended southward almost to the Pyrenees gradually disappeared. The Eurasian lynx headed back out across the continent. For some reason, the Iberian lynx stayed where it was.

Juan Aceituno/Shutterstock

2. **A food and habitat specialist**. Iberian lynxes don't have cyclical swings like the snowshoe hare-loving Canada lynx, but **most of their diet is European rabbits that inhabit southwestern Europe**. That's quite a contrast to Eurasian lynxes, which take almost anything that comes their way. Iberian lynxes also need **dry Mediterranean scrubland**, preferably with a mix of dense thickets for sheltering and open areas where they can hunt. Natural cavities like hollow trees or rock crevices are necessary, too, for raising a family.

3. **From 1996 to 2015, the most endangered cat in the world**. Iberian lynxes went from an estimated 1,000 individuals in 1980 to only 52 in 2002. Precise causes for the decline are still under investigation. Human activities had a lot to do with this, but so did diseases that almost wiped out the local rabbits. Once the enormity of this cat's plight was recognized, a team of government officials, conservationists, academics, and local residents stepped in. Much more needs to be done, but their work thus far has been successful -- the last census, from 2018, found 686 lynxes out there now. These include 241 lynxes reintroduced through programs like the one in Spain that led to this release: https://youtube.com/watch?v=9hR-XYy5QyM . In 2015, Iberian lynxes were downlisted from "Critically Endangered" to "Endangered," but their long-term future still is uncertain. (*Cat Specialist Group; Ferreras et al.; Fundación CBD-Habitat; Macdonald et al.; Rodriguez and Calzada; Wildt et al.*)

Tony Mills/Shutterstock

Data: This information is from the Cat Specialist Group, except where noted.

- **Weight:** 18 to 35 pounds.

- **Height at the shoulder**: 24 to 28 inches. (*Wikipedia*)
- **Body length**: 26 to 36 inches.
- **Tail length**: Roughly 4 to 6 inches.
- **Coat**: Short, thick fur with a tawny background color ranging from yellowish through red and brown to gray. Spots are dark brown or black, with some dark bars, particularly in the Donana National Park region. Belly fur is a lighter color, while a look at online images shows that the beard-like ruff that frames this feline goblin's face is a mix of darker colors and patches of white.

miguellm/Shutterstock

- **Litter size**: 1 to 4, per the Cat Specialist Group, but usually 3 in the wild. (*Wildt et al.*)

Where found in the wild:

For most of the 21st century, wild Iberian lynx only existed in 2 small regions of southwestern Spain: the Andujar-Cardena region and Donana National Park.

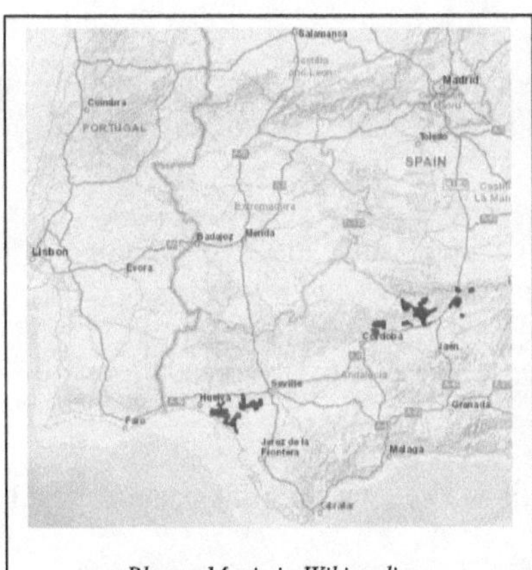
BhagyaMani via Wikimedia, https://commons.wikimedia.org/wiki/File:Iberi anLynx_distribution2015.jpg#mw-jump-to-license CC BY-SA 4.0

Besides building up these very isolated groups through managed breeding and release programs, conservationists also have reintroduced lynx to two new areas.

Over time, they hope to get five more populations going in Spain and Portugal (where the first Iberian lynxes were released in 2014). (*Rodriguez and Calzada*)

Habitat:

- **Range of environments**: Look for Iberian lynx in a mosaic landscape of open areas and stands of native oak with plenty of undergrowth or maquis/chaparral thickets. Observers have seen the cats at elevations of 5,000 feet or more but typically inhabit lands that are 1,300 to 3,000 feet above sea level. (*Cat Specialist Group*)
- **Prey base**: An Iberian lynx may snack on the occasional small mammal, bird, or reptile, but European rabbits make up more than 80% of its diet. Very rarely, Iberian lynxes do take domestic goats and sheep. They have never been known to attack people.

- **Example of guild**: The fossil record shows that, during the last ice age, Iberian lynx shared this refuge with Eurasian lynxes, wildcats, cave lions, and leopards, among other carnivores. Today, the only other wild felines on the peninsula are a few European wildcats that researchers found in Donana National Park; the predator competition there more commonly includes badgers, foxes, mongooses, and genets. (*Fedriani et al.; Sommer and Benecke; Zapata et al.*)

Red-list status:

Intensive efforts have brought the Iberian lynx back from near extinction, yet it is still endangered.

And, while breeding programs and reintroduction have helped a lot, they can't completely alter the fact that Iberian lynxes have the lowest genome-wide genetic diversity of any species reported thus far. (*Abascal et al.*)

In plain English, this means that their "balance" in the genetic "bank" is too low to cope with emergencies such as disease outbreaks or drastic climate change. (*Simpson*)

Conservationists, in their Iberian lynx breeding programs, carefully try to spread around what little genetic diversity remains.

But people can only do so much. We'll just have to wait and see whether this beautiful cat has enough resilience to survive.

Wildcats
(Part of the Felis/domestic cat lineage)

European Wildcats

Bildagentur Zoonar GmbH/Shutterstock

Name: There are wild cats (two words) in the New World but no wildcats (one word) there, except for domesticated ones that accompanied the first European settlers. (Yes, house cats and Old World wildcats are related.)

Wildcats are the Pandora's Box of family Felidae because they all blend into one another (*Heptner and Sludskii*) -- there are few clear-cut differences in any given region that a taxonomist can point to and say "Aha! Separate species!"

*Yet wildcats separated by great distances are obviously different. (Image: **Steppe wildcat** in Africa (left), by Martin Mecnarowski/Shutterstock; **European wildcat** (right), by Tambako the Jaguar, https://www.flickr.com/photos/tambako/25383454413 CC BY-ND 2.0)*

The scientific name for wildcats reflects their common name in many languages: *Felis silvestris*, "forest cat."

But there are all sorts of complications that come with this simple scientific name. Some experts, after reviewing many arcane details, continue to use *F. silvestris* for all wildcats. Others argue that different species names are sometimes necessary.

Fortunately, we don't need to open Pandora's Box. We can simply check out the four traditional groups used for wildcats.

And everyone agrees that the one we're going to look at now -- the European wildcat -- is *Felis silvestris silvestris*.

Imagine family after family, year after year, down through geologic time. (Image of wildcats in Scotland: Peter Trimming, https://www.flickr.com/photos/peter-trimming/5140916394 CC BY 2.0)

Lineage: Domestic cat (a/k/a Felis).

Outstanding Features:

1. **The oldest wildcat species**. (*Cat Specialist Group*) As a group, wildcats are probably descended from *Felis lunensis*, known informally as Martelli's cat. This small predator roamed Europe perhaps as long ago as the late Pliocene epoch. *Felis silvestris* probably appeared during middle Pleistocene times, some 450,000 to 350,000 years ago.

From that point on, Europe remained the center of wildcat evolution until roughly 50,000 years ago. According to fossils, that's when some wildcats moved out of Europe into Africa and Asia Minor -- they were the ancestors of other modern wildcats and, ultimately, the domestic cat. Since there was no land bridge between Europe and North America at that time, wildcats never made it to the New World. (*Heptner and Sludskii; Kurtén; Werdelin et al.; Yamaguchi et al., 2004*)

2. **Hybridization with the domestic cat**. When "cats of the forest" and free-roaming or feral house cats meet, they sometimes interbreed. This has been going on for so long now that there may be very few genetically "original" European wildcats left. (*Cat Specialist Group*) Mattucci *et al.* report extensive hybridization in Scotland and Hungary, while up to 10% of the wildcats in southern and central Europe may be domestic-wild hybrids. But such field research is very difficult. Wildcats are shy and easily avoid trapping for radio-collar and other studies. Simply looking at them isn't helpful -- wildcats, hybrids, and domestic cats closely resemble each other. Much more work on this is needed.

3. **Sicily has the only Mediterranean island population of European wildcats**. Rising sea levels at the end of the last ice age stranded some European wildcats on Sicily. There are also wildcats on other islands, but genetic testing suggests that these are probably descended from feral domestic cats that Neolithic people brought across the sea. (*Mattucci et al.; Yamaguchi et al., 2015*) That's still a pretty awesome history!

Data: This information is from the Cat Specialist Group, except where noted.

- **Weight**: 7 to 18 pounds.

- **Height at the shoulder**: 14 to 16 inches. (*Encyclopaedia Britannica*)

- **Body length**: 18 to 32 inches.

- **Tail length**: 12 inches.

- **Coat**: Just like a tabby cat's (thin tabby stripes, not blotches) but with thicker, longer fur, especially in winter. The stripes are more distinct in the western part of the European wildcat's range, per

"Pfui on your science, hoomans!"--European wildcat.. (Image: Tambako the Jaguar, https://www.flickr.com/photos/tambako/25283 739853 CC BY-ND 2.0

Kitchener *et al.*, 2017. And, as shown in this video of a wildcat scavenging roadkill in Belgium -- https://youtu.be/abv8oc3AFUE -- wildcats have a bushy ringed tail that's tipped in black, as well as a dark line of fur running down the back. No melanistic (all black) wildcats have been recorded in Europe.

- **Vocals:** Much like Fluffy's. (*Sunquist and Sunquist*)

- **Litter size**: 1 to 7. As this video shows, wildcat kittens are just as adorable as Fluffy's: https://youtu.be/a1EjP6p4yV0

Where found in the wild:

This secretive little cat is difficult to find, let alone study.

Some of today's known European wildcat locations are in northern Scotland (here's a camera-trap video in the highlands: https://youtu.be/dpMOTVKBneo), Germany, Luxembourg, France, the Pyrenees, Switzerland, Austria, Belgium, and the Netherlands, as well as in southern and central Europe and neighboring parts of Russia.

Wildcats are absent from the Nordic countries and apparently never inhabited Ireland. They disappeared from England, Wales, and southern Scotland in the mid-19th century.

Habitat:

Tambako the Jaguar,
https://www.flickr.com/photos/tambako/41679
643455 CC BY-ND 2.0

- **Range of environments:**   There's a reason why these are called forest cats, but European wildcats use a variety of habitats with trees, ranging from swamps in the Caucasus Mountains to Carpathian virgin hardwood forest to the arid Mediterranean maqui/chaparral of Italy and southwestern Spain. As long as there is enough cover for hunting and resting, and not more than around 7 inches of snow during the winter, wildcats can adapt to a variety of habitats.
- **Prey base:** Rodents, mainly, though rabbits and hares are also on the menu in Spain and Scotland. European wildcats also take frogs, fish, and other small animals up to the size of a young deer.
- **Example of guild:** This camera trap caught Romania's top five predators: https://youtube.com/watch?v=eirV-v4jngs It's a harsh world out there -- wildcats kill and are killed by other carnivores their size, like weasels, martens, and polecats. They must also avoid lynxes and other large predators.

Red-list status:

The European wildcat is still widespread and abundant enough to be listed as Least Concern. The biggest threat it faces is "cryptic extinction" -- loss of the original wildcat genetic legacy through hybridization with domestic cats.

For more information about wildcats, check out the Cat Specialist Group webpage at http://www.catsg.org/index.php?id=101 and the IUCN assessment at https://www.iucnredlist.org/species/60354712/50652361

Chinese Mountain Cats

ylq/Shutterstock

Name: This rugged little feline is known locally as a "grass cat" -- its fur color blends well into the dry grass of wild Tibet.

Names in the West have included "desert cat" and "Chinese steppe cat," but most people today now call it a Chinese mountain cat. (*He et al.*)

Opinion is divided on the scientific name.

Some authorities consider it a wildcat: *Felis silvestris bieti*, meaning "forest cat," subspecies "bieti." Others think that such a rare kitty might be a separate species: *Felis bieti*.

The arguments behind these opposing views go way over my head. I have included the Chinese mountain cat in this book, rather than the upcoming one on Asian cats, simply because:

1. It looks like a wildcat to me -- especially in this video: https://youtube.com/watch?v=HK5BclSkMEQ -- even if it eventually does turn out to be a separate species.
2. Kitchener *et al.* point out that the Chinese mountain cat could be descended from steppe wildcats that were isolated in Central Asia during the last ice age. If true, this is a slightly closer link to wildcats than to any other Asian cat.

Lineage: There is no disagreement here -- Chinese mountain cats sit on the Felis (domestic cat) branch of the cat-family tree.

Outstanding Features:

1. **One of the least known members of family Felidae**. The existence of Chinese mountain cats has been recognized by Western scientists since the 1880s, but very little information on them was available until the early 21st century. Even today, this little feline is mostly a mystery to native hunters and Chinese scientists alike (*He et al.*), while the IUCN reported in 2015 that there had been no progress in understanding the Chinese mountain cat's status and distribution since the last red-list assessment in 2010. Researchers are still working on it, though. In 2018, they succeeded in getting the first video of a Chinese mountain cat in the wild: https://youtube.com/watch?v=_SQTVIB0lcs
2. **The only cat found in China and nowhere else**. The country's other wild cats, including snow leopards, tigers, and Eurasian lynxes, do cross international borders. Per He *et al.*, most Chinese mountain cats live in Qinghai Province, while historically they were also known in Sichuan. Records in Ningxia, Shaanxi, and Xinjiang provinces are uncertain.
3. **Enlarged ears and related internal structures**. This rather arcane anatomic detail comes about because sound doesn't carry very well in dry air. That's a problem for both predators and prey. To get around it, many small mammals from arid climates have evolved extra-large external and internal hearing equipment. This is why Chinese mountain cat inner ear structures are larger than those of most other cats.
4. **They live in burrows**. The best shelter from wind and cold in Tibet is underground. I don't know if Chinese mountain cats excavate their own or take over a prey's hidey-hole. They are good diggers -- people have observed them listening for a mole rat's movements underground and then tunneling down in after it. But small cats do often co-opt a prey animal's burrow.

Data: This information is from the Cat Specialist Group, except where noted.

- **Weight**: 12 to 20 pounds. Chinese mountain cats are small compared to, say, snow leopards, but they're still twice the size of a house cat.
- **Height at the shoulder**: Almost 10 inches. (*Tibet Nature*)
- **Body length**: 24 to 34 inches.
- **Tail length**: About 11 to 14 inches.

- **Coat**: The summer coat is dark brown, with paler underparts and darker hind feet; in winter, fur thickens and turns a light gray/ocher, though underparts remains white to pale yellow. There is faint brown horizontal striping on the sides and legs, as well as one stripe on each cheek. The Chinese mountain cat's large ears are yellow-gray on the back and have dark brown tufts, somewhat like a lynx but not as long. Its ringed tail has a black tip, and there is some long hair in between the toes, though not as much as on the desert-dwelling sand cat. (*Cat Specialist Group; Sunquist and Sunquist; Tibet Nature*)
- **Litter size**: 2 to 4 (this is probably from the very few cats in zoos; next to nothing is known of the Chinese mountain cat's life in the wild)

Where found in the wild:

Chinese mountain cats have only been reported from the northeastern and eastern edge of the Tibet Plateau -- that's the "mountain" part of their name.

As mentioned above, details of the "Chinese" part are more uncertain because it is so poorly known. (*He et al.*)

Qinghai Province appears to be the mountain cat's stronghold -- it's mostly rural, with people and industry concentrated mainly in the capital city of Xining. (*He et al.*)

Habitat:

- **Range of environments**: Like their snow leopard neighbors, Chinese mountain cats apparently dwell only in the high country, where they experience harsh climate extremes. Their small size limits them to relatively snow-free areas, mainly alpine meadows between 8,000 and 16,500 feet. Chinese mountain cats have not yet been recorded in deserts or dense forests.
- **Prey base**: Rodents, mostly voles, rats, and pikas. Chinese mountain cats probably also scavenge as well as take the occasional bird and lagomorph (various relatives of the rabbit).
- **Example of guild**: Chinese mountain cats and steppe wildcats may overlap a bit in some parts of their respective ranges. (*MacDonald et al.*) Otherwise, it's difficult to find information about other small carnivores in Chinese mountain cat country. Large predators include jackals and Eurasian lynx, as well as snow leopards, per this video -- https://youtube.com/watch?v=knAgVAdf9dA .

Red-list status:

Vulnerable, but the status of this rare cat is uncertain, like so much else about it (*Riordan et al.*).

For more information about Chinese mountain cats and the threats they face, check out the latest IUCN assessment at https://www.iucnredlist.org/species/8539/50651398 , as well as the Cat Specialist Group's species page at http://www.catsg.org/index.php?id=104 .

Steppe Wildcats

EcoPrint at Shutterstock

Name: These are descendants of wildcats who left Europe's forests some 50,000 years ago, heading south into Africa and eastward into Asia Minor.

Along the way, they slimmed down and developed shorter fur and longer legs, among other changes. A common name for them now is steppe or bush wildcats, because that's the sort of landscape they live in.

Other names are based on geography -- African wildcat; Arabian wildcat; Indian desert cat; Asian wildcat (not the same thing as a Chinese mountain cat); and so forth.

Their scientific names are controversial.

Ornata resembles its two African relatives but it's a little smaller and has spots. (Image: Raja Bandi via https://commons.wikimedia.org/wiki/File:Felis _silvestris_ornata.jpg#mw-jump-to-license Wikimedia, CC BY-SA 4.0)

Traditionally, steppe wildcats are known as:

- *Lybica*: Those in northern Africa and the Near East
- *Cafra*: Wildcats in southern Africa up to around Mozambique or Tanzania, per the Cat Specialist Group
- *Ornata*: Southwestern and central Asian wildcats

The question is whether these are **wildcat subspecies** or a separate **"Lybica group"** -- still wildcats, but no longer closely resembling their European wildcat ancestor.

Since we're not taxonomists, let's just say that there can be different scientific names for a steppe wildcat.

In every case, 3 names -- for genus, species, and subspecies -- are used.

But:

- if the authority you're consulting agrees with the **"wildcat subspecies"** argument, like Driscoll *et al.*, then those 3 scientific names will be *Felis silvestris* (*lybica, cafra,* or *ornata*).

- if they prefer the **"Lybica group"** hypothesis, like Kitchener *et al.*, then expect to see *Felis lybica* (*lybica, cafra,* or *ornata*).

Lineage: Felis (a/k/a domestic cat).

Outstanding Features:

1. **Longer legs, shorter fur, and a sleeker, more supple build than the European wildcat.** During the last 50,000 years, steppe wildcats lost their rugged cold-weather, forest-dependent characteristics and evolved into warmth-loving felines who are quite agile in open, rocky terrain. They also need long legs to hunt prey in grass -- these give steppe wildcats a very distinctive look (I think the cats shown in this video are Cafra: https://youtu.be/PHCOjXKFz9A)
2. **More tolerant of people than European wildcats are.** Steppe wildcats sometimes approach settlements and even live on the fringes of our cities. They also hunt in pastures and other cultivated areas. European wildcats will occasionally venture into human-altered land, too, but they are wary and always stay close to the forest's edge.

3. Genetic tests, archaeological finds, and Ancient Egyptian art all show that **African wildcats are the ancestors of modern house cats**. Since European wildcats are fierce and hardly to be tamed, cat lovers today are fortunate that it was the more sociable Lybica who inhabited the right place (Fertile Crescent) at the right time (some 9,000 to 10,000 years ago) to meet early farmers and develop a close working/social partnership with humanity that has continued into today.

African wild cat, by Martin Mecnarowski/Shutterstock /Ancient Egyptian Statue, Walters Art Museum via Wikimedia, https://commons.wikimedia.org/wiki/File:Egyptian_-_Statuette_of_a_Cat_-_Walters_542130_-_Three_Quarter.jpg public domain.

Data: This information is from the Cat Specialist Group, except where noted.

- **Weight**: African wildcats (***Lybica/Cafra***): 6.6 to 18 pounds; Asiatic wildcat (***Ornata***): 4.4 to 17 pounds.

- **Body length**: *Lybica/Cafra*: 18 to 32 inches; *Ornata*: 16 to 25 inches

- **Tail length**: *Lybica/Cafra*: 12 inches; *Ornata*: 8.6 to 15 inches.

- **Coat**: The background color on all steppe wildcats ranges from gray to reddish brown. ***Lybica and Cafra*** sport dark tabby stripes. (This genetic heritage, by the way, is why all domestic cats, even solid-colored ones, are tabbies -- many of them have color mutations that either conceal the stripes or actually turn off the tabby gene.) ***Ornata*** is the spotted steppe wildcat. Its fur is typically paler than an African wildcat's, and its spots are small, sometimes coalescing into dark stripes on the legs and tail. (*Sunquist and Sunquist*) All steppe wildcat tails are more slender and tapering than the European wildcat's but do have the same rings and dark tip.

- **Vocals:** Just like Fluffy.

- **Litter size:** *Lybica/Cafra*: 1 to 6; *Ornata*: 2 to 4, rarely up to 8.

Where found in the wild:

- Look for **Lybica** in eastern, western, and northern Africa; the Arabian Peninsula and other parts of the Near East. Wildcats on the Mediterranean islands of Corsica, Sardinia, and Crete, resemble African wildcats, but they're probably descendants of feral domestic cats that Neolithic people brought with them. (*Macdonald et al., 2010b*)

- **Cafra** prowls through southern Africa -- the border with Lybica's range might be in Mozambique or Tanzania. (*Cat Specialist Group*)

- **Ornata** lives in southwestern and central Asia, including Iran, Afghanistan, Pakistan, India, Mongolia, and China. Per Kitchener *et al.*, it's possible that an Ornata subpopulation was isolated in Central Asia during the last ice age and eventually evolved into the Chinese mountain cat.

Habitat:

- **Range of environments:**   In both Africa and Asia, steppe wildcats have been seen as high as 10,000 feet, but they're more common at lower elevations. ***Lybica and Cafra*** adapt to almost any African habitat except the tropical rainforest. In the Sahara and Arabian deserts, though, they only live on mountains or along dry waterways. ***Ornata***, on the other hand (paw?), avoids both desert and dense forest, preferring cover and at least a little nearby water. It's usually seen in places like semi-desert scrub, temperate forests, and mountain woodlands. (*Cat Specialist Group*)

- **Prey base:** Mainly rodents, including rats, mice, voles, jerboas, and gerbils. However, birds often supplement the diet, and both African and Asian wildcats occasionally take other small animals up to the size of a lamb or young antelope. (*Cat Specialist Group*) Here is a video of Cafra hunting: https://www.youtube.com/watch?v=sHvMQI8p5zQ

- **Example of guild: Asia**: In the western part of its range, ***Ornata*** must cope with predators like cheetahs, leopards, brown bears, and wolves; in the east, Ornata and the Chinese mountain cat ranges may overlap, though this hasn't been proven yet. **Africa**: There are wildcats out on the Serengeti; they must keep a low profile in holes dug by warthogs and other animals to escape the big cats and other large predators. However, ***Lybica and Cafra*** are the largest members of Africa's small predator guild, which may give them dominance over sand cats and black-footed cats, as well as other carnivores like mongooses, genets, polecats, and meerkats. (*Ghoddousi et al.; Herbst; Macdonald et al., 2010a; de Satge et al.; Sunquist and Sunquist*)

Red-list status:

This is a little tricky, since steppe wildcats and Fluffy -- the most widespread and abundant of all cats -- are so closely related.

Also, wildcats and domestic cats interbreed in Africa and Asia. Thanks to this hybridization, no one is sure just how many "pure" steppe wildcats there are nowadays.

The International Union for Conservation of Nature and Natural Resources (IUCN) lists wildcats as Least Concern, but it has not yet done a separate review of steppe/bush wildcats.

Check out the Cat Specialist Group's pages on African wildcats at
http://www.catsg.org/index.php?id=112 and Asian wildcats at
http://www.catsg.org/index.php?id=102 for more information.

The Domestic Cat

"Was the trade-off worth it?" John Pemble https://www.flickr.com/photos/ambientjohn/8292828262 CC BY-ND 2.0.

Name: The Roman word "cattus" might have come from "kaddiska," a very old North African Berber word for cats.

As for Fluffy's scientific name, some experts say that Fluffy is a species -- *Felis catus*. Others disagree, pointing out that we really haven't changed the wildcat all that much, as we did when domesticating wolves tens of thousands of years ago.

The underlying problem is that we let a cuddly little rodent-killer in from the cold several thousand years

Jaine,
https://www.flickr.com/photos/team_716_pwns
/4170860954 CC BY-ND 2.0

ago and encouraged it to continue acting naturally.

Since then, house cats have changed some of their wild ways, but few of them, outside the cat fancy, appear to be completely domesticated. Herding cows is easy; herding cats? Not so much.

If not a species in its own right, then Fluffy is either a wildcat (*Felis silvestris*) or a wildcat subspecies (*Felis silvestris catus*).

But that's problematical, too, as Macdonald *et al.* point out. Legislation to protect wildcats is written for *Felis silvestris*. No one wants to add house cats to the Red List, but we can't take *Felis silvestris* off the list.

What other option is there but to stick a *Felis catus* label on some of the African wildcats? But that's not allowed under the rules of taxonomy.

Figuring out a proper scientific name for domestic cats is currently giving the boffins a really big headache!

Lineage: Felis (domestic cat).

Outstanding Features:

Lovin Cat,
https://www.flickr.com/photos/lovinkat/208348
79108 CC BY 2.0

1. **Domestication**. You can tame a cheetah or some other wild cat, but its cubs will also need taming. Here's a point for the experts who consider Fluffy a unique species -- they're born domestic. Kittens can bond closely with us, especially if they are handled well early in life.

2. **A wider variety of looks than any other cat**. For almost two centuries, cat breeders have been practicing artificial selection to get the feline rainbow that surrounds us today. Natural selection doesn't necessarily favor such mutations -- for example, Siamese points or the beautifully shaded coat colors of chinchilla and smoke cat breeds. In the wild, some of these gene changes, like rexed or hairless cats, would quickly eliminate the carrier!

3. **The most widespread cat in the world**. This, too, is on us. People took the domestic cat out of the Middle East, where it originated, and brought it with them all across the globe, including places that had never seen cats before, like Australia, New Zealand, and Antarctica.

4. **A lion in our living room**. It's a trite phrase but true. House cats still eat, hunt, and behave like any other cat. And, believe it or not, there isn't much anatomical difference under the skin between Fluffy and a lion or tiger, other than size. (*Turner and Antón*)

Data:

No "typical" information is available on domestic cats. There's just too much variety.

Where found in the wild:

Nowhere (unless you take the "wildcat" viewpoint)..

Feral cats are not wild. They still show signs of domestication (sometimes to the point of being unable to survive in the wild and/or raise young); they tend to stay near people even when they can't tolerate close contact; and their kittens can live happy domestic lives if adopted early enough in life.

Habitat:

- **Range of environments**: Like their wildcat relatives, house cats are very adaptable. That's why they have been able to accompany us throughout the world.

- **Prey base**: In any human-controlled environment, domestic cats are the dominant mesocarnivore (the food-web tier just under that of apex predators like the lion). That's not surprising, since their efficiency at killing rodents and other pests is why we started keeping cats in the first place (the modern focus on appearance is a recent phenomenon). Their effect on local wildlife today is controversial (here is something I wrote about this in 2018: https://flighttowonder.com/2018/04/10/cats-v-wildlife-wheres-the-middle-ground/)

- **Example of guild**: Domestic carnivores are a special case. Few studies have been done, but for an example, here's a paper describing interactions among cats, dogs, and red foxes in Poland: https://www.nrcresearchpress.com/doi/full/10.1139/cjz-2012-0072

Red-list status:

Not listed (unless you subscribe to the "wildcat" hypothesis).

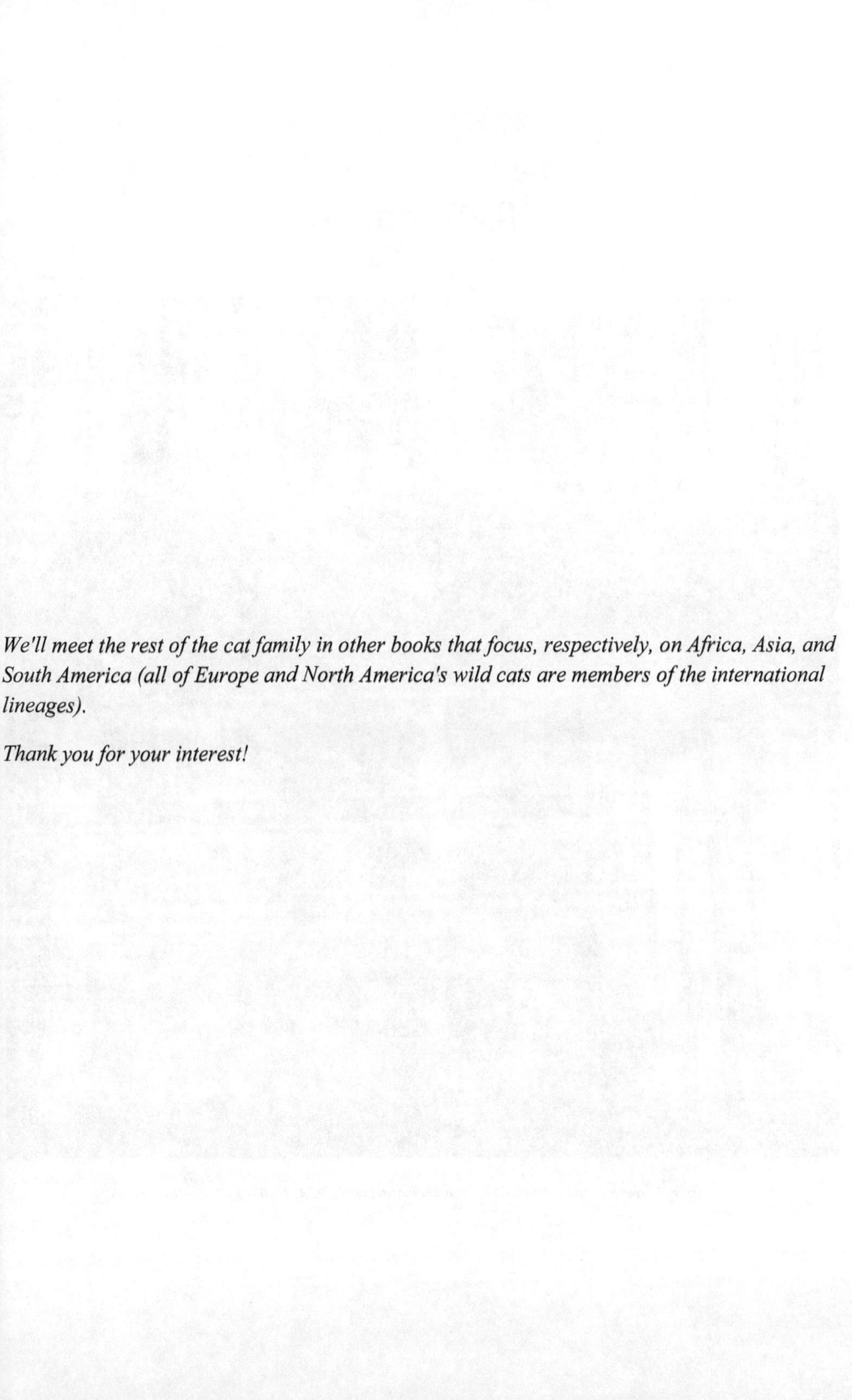

We'll meet the rest of the cat family in other books that focus, respectively, on Africa, Asia, and South America (all of Europe and North America's wild cats are members of the international lineages).

Thank you for your interest!

References

Bauer, H.; Packer, C.; Funston, P.F.; Henschel, P.; and Nowell, K. 2016. *Panthera leo (errata version published in 2017). The IUCN Red List of Threatened Species 2016: e.T15951A115130419. https://www.iucnredlist.org/species/15951/115130419*

Bocherens, H. 2015. *Isotopic tracking of large carnivore palaeoecology in the mammoth steppe. Quaternary Science Reviews, 117: 42-71.*

Breitenmoser, U.; Mallon, D.P.; Ahmad Khan, J.; and Driscoll, C. 2008. *Panthera leo ssp. persica. The IUCN Red List of Threatened Species 2008: e.T15952A5327221. https://www.iucnredlist.org/species/15952/5327221*

Cat Specialist Group. 2019. **African lion**. *http://www.catsg.org/index.php?id=108 Last accessed March 5, 2019.*

___. 2019. **Asiatic lion**. *http://www.catsg.org/index.php?id=113 Last accessed March 5, 2019.*

Christiansen, P. 2008. *Phylogeny of the great cats (Felidae: Pantherinae), and the influence of fossil taxa and missing characters. Cladistics, 24(6): 977-992.*

Cincinnati Zoo & Botanical Garden. 2019. *White lion. http://cincinnatizoo.org/animals/white-lion-2/ Last accessed October 24, 2019.*

Craft, M. E. 2010. *Ecology of infectious diseases in Serengeti lions, in Biology and Conservation of Wild Felids, ed. Macdonald, D. W., and Loveridge, A. J., 263-281. Oxford: Oxford University Press.*

Ewer, R. F. 1973. *The carnivores. The World Naturalist, ed. Carrington, R. London: Weidenfeld and Nicolson.*

Figueiró, H. V.; Li, G.; Trindade, F. J.; Assis, J.; and others. 2017. *Genome-wide signatures of complex introgression and adaptive evolution in the big cats. Science Advances, 3(7): e1700299.*

Hayward, M. W., and Slotow, R. 2009. *Temporal partitioning of activity in large African carnivores: tests of multiple hypotheses. African Journal of Wildlife Research, 39(2): 109-126.*

Johnson, W. E.; Eizirik, E.; Pecon-Slattery, J.; Murphy, W. J.; and others. 2006. *The Late Miocene radiation of modern Felidae: A genetic assessment. Science, 311: 73-77.*

King, L. M. 2012. *Phylogeny of Panthera, Including P. atrox, Based on Cranialmandibular Characters. Electronic Theses and Dissertations. Paper 1444. http://dc.etsu.edu/etd/1444*

Kitchener, A. C.; Van Valkenburgh, B.; and Yamaguchi, N. 2010. *Felid form and function, in Biology and Conservation of Wild Felids, ed. Macdonald, D. W., and Loveridge, A. J., 83-106. Oxford: Oxford University Press.*

Kitchener, A. C.; Breitenmoser-Würsten, C.; Eizirik, E.; Gentry, A.; and others. 2017. *A revised taxonomy of the Felidae: The final report of the Cat Classification Task Force of the IUCN Cat Specialist Group. https://repository.si.edu/bitstream/handle/10088/32616/A_revised_Felidae_Taxonomy_CatNews.pdf*

Li, G.; Davis, B. W.; Eizirik, E.; and Murphy, W. J. 2016. *Phylogenomic evidence for ancient hybridization in the genomes of living cats (Felidae). Genome Research, 26(1): 1-11.*

Loveridge, A.; Wang, S. W.; Frank, L.; and Seidensticker, J. 2010. *People and wild felids: conservation of cats and management of conflicts, in Biology and Conservation of Wild Felids, eds. Macdonald, D. W., and Loveridge, A. J., 161-195. Oxford: Oxford University Press.*

Loveridge, A. J.; Hemson, G.; Davidson, Z.; and Macdonald, D. W. 2010a. *African lions on the edge: reserve boundaries as 'attractive sinks', in Biology and Conservation of Wild Felids, eds. Macdonald, D. W., and Loveridge, A. J., 283-304. Oxford: Oxford University Press.*

Macdonald, D. W.; Loveridge, A. J.; and Nowell, K. 2010a. *Dramatis personae: An introduction to the wild felids, in Biology and Conservation of Wild Felids, eds. Macdonald, D. W., and Loveridge, A. J., 3-58. Oxford: Oxford University Press.*

Macdonald, D. W;, Mosser, A.; and Gittleman, J. L. 2010b. *Felid society, in Biology and Conservation of Wild Felids, eds. Macdonald, D. W., and Loveridge, A. J., 125-160. Oxford: Oxford University Press.*

Macdonald, D. W.; Loveridge, A. J.; and Rabinowitz, A. 2010c. *Felid futures: crossing disciplines, borders, and generations, in Biology and Conservation of Wild Felids, eds. Macdonald, D. W., and Loveridge, A. J., 599. Oxford: Oxford University Press.*

Motsinger, C. 2018. *Two of the rarest animals in the planet are in Cincinnati. But maybe not for long. https://www.cincinnati.com/story/news/2018/09/26/cincinnati-zoo-home-maybe-oldest-white-lions-earth/1283501002/ Last accessed October 24, 2019.*

National Sleep Foundation. 2019. *These kings of the jungle get quite a bit of shut-eye! https://www.sleep.org/articles/sleep-habits-of-lions/ Last accessed October 24, 2019.*

Nyakatura, K., and Bininda-Emonds, O. R. P. 2012. *Updating the evolutionary history of Carnivora (Mammalia): a new species-level supertree complete with divergence time estimates. BMC Biology. 10:12.*

O'Brien, S. J., and Johnson, W. E. 2007. *The evolution of cats. Scientific American, 297 (1): 68-75..*

Stuart, A. J. 2015. *Late Quaternary megafaunal extinctions on the continents: a short review. Geological Journal, 50(3): 338-363.*

Sunquist, M. and Sunquist, F. 2002. *Wild Cats of the World. Chicago and London: University of Chicago Press. Retrieved from https://play.google.com/store/books/details?id=IF8nDwAAQBAJ*

Turner, A., and Antón, M. 1997. *The Big Cats and Their Fossil Relatives: An Illustrated Guide to Their Evolution and Natural History. New York: Columbia University Press.*

Werdelin, L.; Yamaguchi, N.; Johnson, W. E.; and O'Brien, S. J.. 2010. *Phylogeny and evolution of cats (Felidae), in Biology and Conservation of Wild Felids, eds. Macdonald, D. W., and Loveridge, A. J., 59-82. Oxford: Oxford University Press.*

Werdelin, L., and Dehghani, R. 2011. *Carnivora, in Paleontology and Geology of Laetoli: Human Evolution in Context, Volume 2: Fossil Hominins and the Associated Fauna, Harrison, T., ed., 189-232. Springer, Dordrecht.*

Wikipedia. 2019. *Lion. https://en.wikipedia.org/wiki/Lion Last accessed October 25, 2019.*

___. 2019. *White lion. https://en.wikipedia.org/wiki/White_lion Last accessed October 24, 2019.*

Allen, W. L.; Cuthill, I. C.; Scott-Samuel, N. E.; and Baddeley, R. 2011. *Why the leopard got its spots: relating pattern development to ecology in felids. Proceedings of the Royal Society B,* 278: 1373-1380.

Amur Tiger Center. 2018. *Saving Russian Heritage Together (Russian and English) http://amur-tiger.ru/data/report-2018.pdf*

Animal Fair. 2015. *Las Vegas Icons Siegfried And Roy – Where Are The Tigers Now? https://animalfair.com/2015/10/19/siegfried-roy-tigers-now/ Last accessed October 29, 2019.*

Cat Specialist Group. 2019. *Tiger. http://www.catsg.org/index.php?id=124 Last accessed May 17, 2019.*

Cho, Y. S.; Hu, L.; Hou, H.; Lee, H.; and others. 2013. *The tiger genome and comparative analysis with lions and snow leopard genomes. Nature Communications, 4: 24-33.*

Chowdhury, A. N.; Brahma, A.; Mondal, R.; and Biswas, M. K. 2016. *Stigma of tiger attack: Study of tiger-widows from Sundarban Delta, India. Journal of Indian Psychiatry, 58(1): 12-19.*

Chundawat, R. S.; Khan, J. A.; and Mallon, D. P. 2011. *Panthera tigris ssp. tigris. The IUCN Red List of Threatened Species 2011:e.T136899A4348945.*

Christiansen, P. 2008. *Phylogeny of the great cats (Felidae: Pantherinae), and the influence of fossil taxa and missing characters. Cladistics, 24(6): 977-992.*

Culver, M.; Driscoll, C.; Eizirik, E.; and Spong, G. 2010. *Genetic applications in wild felids, in Biology and Conservation of Wild Felids, ed. Macdonald, D. W., and Loveridge, A. J., 107-124. Oxford: Oxford University Press.*

Das, C. S. 2018. *Pattern and characterisation of human casualties in Sundarban by tiger attacks, India. Sustainable Forestry, 1(2):1-10.*

Davis, B. W.; Li, G.; and Murphy. W. J. 2010. *Supermatrix and species tree methods resolve phylogenetic relationships within the big cats, Panthera (Carnivora: Felidae). Molecular Phylogenetics and Evolution, 56(1): 64-76.*

Dhungana, R.; Savini, T.; Karki, J. B.; Dhakal, M.; and others. 2018. *Living with tigers Panthera tigris: patterns, correlates, and contexts of human– tiger conflict in Chitwan National Park, Nepal. Oryx, 52(1): 55-65.*

Ewer, R. F. 1973. *The carnivores. The World Naturalist, ed. Carrington, R. London: Weidenfeld and Nicolson.*

Godfrey, D.; Lythgoe, J. N.; and Rumball, D. A. 1987. *Zebra stripes and tiger stripes: the spatial frequency distribution of the pattern compared to that of the background is significant in display and crypsis. Biological Journal of the Linnaean Society, 32(4): 427-433.*

Goodrich, J.; Lynam, A.; Miguelle, D.; Wibisono, H.; and others. 2015. *Panthera tigris. The IUCN Red List of Threatened Species 2015:3.T15955A50659951.*

Goswami, U. 2019. *View: Doubling tiger population laudable but India needs to do more. https://economictimes.indiatimes.com/news/science/view-doubling-tiger-population-laudable-but-india-needs-to-do-more/articleshow/70435503.cms?from=mdr Last accessed October 29, 2019.*

Haslam, M., and Petraglia, M. 2010. *Comment on "Environmental impact of the 73 ka Toba super-eruption in South Asia" by MAJ Williams, SH Ambrose, S. van der Kaars, C. Ruehlemann, U. Chattopadhyaya, J. Pal and PR Chauhan [Palaeogeography, Palaeoclimatology, Palaeoecology 284 (2009) 295– 314]. Palaeogeography, Palaeoclimatology, Palaeoecology, 296(1-2): 199-203.*

Heptner, V. G., and Sludskii, A. A. 1972. *Mammals of the Soviet Union, volume II, part 2: Carnivora (hyaenas and cats).* Moscow: Vysshaya Shkola Publishers. English translation by Rao, P., 1992. General editor: Kothekar, V. S. New Delhi: Amerind Publishing. https://archive.org/details/mammalsofsov221992gept

Herbst, M. 2009. *Behavioural ecology and population genetics of the African wild cat, Felis silvestris Forster 1870, in the southern Kalahari.* PhD thesis, University of Pretoria.

Heske, E. J. Fall 2013 semester. *Mammalogy 462, online class notes. Carnivora Suborder Feliformia* http://www.life.illinois.edu/ib/462/Lab%2019%20Carnivora1.pdf Last accessed October 30, 2019.

Johnson, W. E.; Eizirik, E.; Pecon-Slattery, J.; Murphy, W. J.; and others. 2006. *The Late Miocene radiation of modern Felidae: A enetic assessment.* Science, 311: 73-77.

Kitchener, A. C., Van Valkenburgh, B., and Yamaguchi, N. 2010. *Felid form and function. In Biology and Conservation of Wild Felids,* ed. Macdonald, D. W. and Loveridge, A. J., 83-106. Oxford: Oxford University Press, Oxford.

Kitchener, A. C., and Yamaguchi, N. 2010. *What is a tiger? Biogeography, morphology, and taxonomy, in Tigers of the World* (pp. 53-84). William Andrew Publishing.

Kitchener, A. C.; Breitenmoser-Würsten, C.; Eizirik, E.; Gentry, A.; and others. 2017. *A revised taxonomy of the Felidae: The final report of the Cat Classification Task Force of the IUCN Cat Specialist Group.* https://repository.si.edu/bitstream/handle/10088/32616/A_revised_Felidae_Taxonomy_CatNews.pdf

Kupferschmidt, K. 2015. *Controversial study claims there are only two types of tigers.* https://www.sciencemag.org/news/2015/06/controversial-study-claims-there-are-only-two-types-tiger Last accessed November 6, 2019.

Linkie, M.; Wibisono, H. T.; Martyr, D. J.; and Sunarto, S. 2008. *Panthera tigris ssp. sumatrae. The IUCN Red List of Threatened Species 2008:e.T15966A5334836.* https://www.iucnredlist.org/species/15966/5334836

Louys, J. 2012. *Mammal community structure of Sundanese fossil assemblages from the Late Pleistocene, and a discussion on the ecological effects of the Toba eruption. Quaternary International,* 258: 80-87.

Loveridge, A.; Wang, S. W.; Frank, L.; and Seidensticker, J. 2010. *People and wild felids: conservation of cats and management of conflicts, in Biology and Conservation of Wild Felids,* eds. Macdonald, D. W., and Loveridge, A. J., 161-195. Oxford: Oxford University Press.

Luo, S. J.; Kim, J. H.; Johnson, W. E.; Van Der Walt, J.; and others. 2004. *Phylogeography and genetic ancestry of tigers (Panthera tigris). PLoS Biology,* 2(12): e442.

Luo, S-J., and Xu, X. 2014. *Save the White Tigers. Scientific American,* https://www.scientificamerican.com/article/save-the-white-tigers/ Last accessed November 6, 2019.

Macdonald, D. W.; Loveridge, A. J.; and Nowell, K. 2010. *Dramatis personae: An introduction to the wild felids, in Biology and Conservation of Wild Felids,* eds. Macdonald, D. W., and Loveridge, A. J., 3-58. Oxford: Oxford University Press.

Macdonald, D. W;, Mosser, A.; and Gittleman, J. L. 2010a. *Felid society, in Biology and Conservation of Wild Felids,* eds. Macdonald, D. W., and Loveridge, A. J., 125-160. Oxford: Oxford University Press.

Macdonald, D. W.; Loveridge, A. J.; and Rabinowitz, A. 2010b. *Felid futures: crossing disciplines, borders, and generations, in Biology and Conservation of Wild Felids,* eds. Macdonald, D. W., and Loveridge, A. J., 599. Oxford: Oxford University Press.

Mazák, J. H. 2010. *Craniometric variation in the tiger (Panthera tigris): Implications for patterns of diversity, taxonomy and conservation. Mammalian Biology-Zeitschrift für Säugetierkunde,* 75(1): 45-68.

Mazak, J. H. 2010a. *What is Panthera palaeosinensis?. Mammal Review,* 40(1): 90-102.

Mazák, J. H.; Christiansen, P.; and Kitchener, A. C. 2012 Correction: Oldest Known Pantherine Skull and Evolution of the Tiger. PLOS ONE 7(1): 10.1371/annotation/a60b7ac3-7f06-465b-a8df-2f359d59a021.

Miquelle, D. G.; Goodrich, J. M.; Smirnov, E. N.; Stephens, P. A.; and others. 2010. The Amur tiger: a case study of living on the edge, in Biology and Conservation of Wild Felids, eds. Macdonald, D. W., and Loveridge, A. J., 325-339. Oxford: Oxford University Press.

Nyakatura, K., and Bininda-Emonds, O. R. P. 2012. Updating the evolutionary history of Carnivora (Mammalia): a new species-level supertree complete with divergence time estimates. BMC Biology, 10:12.

O'Brien, S. J., and Johnson, W. E. 2005. Big cat genomics. Annual Review of Genomics and Human Genetics. 6:407-429.

O'Brien, S. J., and Johnson, W. E. 2007. The evolution of cats. Scientific American. 297 (1):68-75.

Oñoz-Wright, A. 2015. Siegfried & Roy welcome four tiger cubs. https://blog.vegas.com/las-vegas-attractions/siegfried-roy-welcome-four-tiger-cubs-60811/ Last accessed October 29, 2019.

Sanderson, E.; Forrest, J.; Loucks, C.; Ginsberg, J.; and others. 2010. "Setting priorities for conservation and recovery of wild tigers: 2005-2015. The technical assessment." in Tigers of the world: the science, politics, and conservation of Panthera tigris, edited by Tilson, Ronald Lewis and Nyhus, Philip J., Second ed. 143– 161. New York: Elsevier/Academic Press. Downloaded from https://repository.si.edu/handle/10088/11080

Schneider, A.; Henegar, C.; Day, K.; Absher, D.; and others. 2015. Recurrent evolution of melanism in South American felids. PLoS Genetics. 11(2): e1004892.

Seidensticker, J.; Dinerstein, E.; Goyal, S. P.; Gurung, B.; and others. 2010. Tiger range collapse and recovery at the base of the Himalayas, in Biology and Conservation of Wild Felids, eds. Macdonald, D. W., and Loveridge, A. J., 305-324. Oxford: Oxford University Press.

St. Petersburg Declaration (English). 2010. http://cmsdata.iucn.org/downloads/st_petersburg_declaration_english.pdf

Sunquist, M. and Sunquist, F. 2002. Wild Cats of the World. Chicago and London: University of Chicago Press. Retrieved from https://play.google.com/store/books/details?id=IF8nDwAAQBAJ

Steinmetz, R.; Seuaturien, N.; and Chutipong, W. 2013. Tigers, leopards, and dholes in a half-empty forest: assessing species interactions in a guild of threatened carnivores. Biological Vonservation: 163, 68-78. (Abstract only)

Thakur, J. February 3, 2017. In Sunderbans, no one cares about villagers who go missing in animal attacks. http://www.hindustantimes.com/india-news/in-sunderbans-no-one-cares-about-villagers-who-go-missing-in-animal-attacks/story-qBfi3zcR9OnU0EZXNgGNyJ.html Last accessed September 13, 2017.

Tseng, Z. J.; Wang, X.; Slater, G. J.; Takeuchi, G. T.; and others. 2014. Himalayan fossils of the oldest known pantherine establish ancient origin of big cats. Proceedings of the Royal Society B: Biological Sciences, 281(1774): 20132686.

Turner, A., and Antón, M. 1997. The Big Cats and Their Fossil Relatives: An Illustrated Guide to Their Evolution and Natural History. New York: Columbia University Press.

Wang, S. W., and Macdonald, D. W. 2009. Feeding habits and niche partitioning in a predator guild composed of tigers, leopards and dholes in a temperate ecosystem in central Bhutan. Journal of Zoology, 277(4): 275-283. (Abstract only)

Werdelin, L., and Olsson, L. 1997. How the leopard got its spots: a phylogenetic view off the evolution of felid coat patterns. Biological Journal of the Linnaean Society. 62: 383-400

Werdelin, L.; Yamaguchi, N.; Johnson, W. E.; and O'Brien, S. J. *2010. Phylogeny and evolution of cats (Felidae), in Biology and Conservation of Wild Felids, eds. Macdonald, D. W., and Loveridge, A. J., 59-82. Oxford: Oxford University Press.*

Wikipedia. *2019.* **Captive white tigers.** *https://en.wikipedia.org/wiki/Captive_white_tigers Last accessed November 6, 2019.*

___. *2019.* **Siegfried & Roy.** *https://en.wikipedia.org/wiki/Siegfried_%26_Roy Last accessed October 24, 2019.*

___. *2019.* **Tiger.** *https://en.wikipedia.org/wiki/Tiger Last accessed October 26, 2019.*

___. *2019.* **Tiger conservation.** *https://en.wikipedia.org/wiki/Tiger_conservation Last accessed October 29, 2019.*

Williams, M. A.; Ambrose, S. H.; van der Kaars, S.; Ruehlemann, C.; and others. *2009. Environmental impact of the 73 ka Toba super-eruption in South Asia. Palaeogeography, Palaeoclimatology, Palaeoecology, 284(3-4): 295-314.*

World Wildlife Fund. *2018. Nepal set to become the first country to double its tigers. https://www.worldwildlife.org/press-releases/nepal-set-to-become-first-country-to-double-wild-tiger-population Last accessed October 29, 2019.*

Xu, X.; Dong, G. X.; Hu, X. S.; Miao, L.; and others. *2013. The genetic basis of white tigers. CurrentBbiology, 23(11): 1031-1035.*

Allen, W. L.; Cuthill, I. C.; Scott-Samuel, N. E.; and Baddeley, R. 2011. *Why the leopard got its spots: relating pattern development to ecology in felids. Proceedings of the Royal Society B, 278: 1373-1380.*

Athreya, V.; Odden, M.; Linnell, J. D.; and Karanth, K. U. 2011. *Translocation as a tool for mitigating conflict with leopards in human-dominated landscapes of India. Conservation Biology, 25(1): 133-141.*

Barnosky, A. D.; Koch, P. L.; Feranec, R. S.; Wing, S. L.; and Shabel, A. B. 2004. *Assessing the causes of late Pleistocene extinctions on the continents. Science, 306(5693): 70-75.*

Cat Specialist Group. 2019. *Leopard. http://www.catsg.org/index.php?id=110 Last accessed August 14, 2019.*

Davis, B. W.; Li, G.; and Murphy. W. J. 2010. *Supermatrix and species tree methods resolve phylogenetic relationships within the big cats, Panthera (Carnivora: Felidae). Molecular Phylogenetics and Evolution, 56(1): 64-76.*

Eizirik, E.; Yuhki, N.; Johnson, W. E.; Menotti-Raymond, M.; and others. 2003. *Molecular genetics and evolution of melanism in the cat family. Current Biology, 13(5): 448-453.*

Ewer, R. F. 1973. *The carnivores. The World Naturalist, ed. Carrington, R. London: Weidenfeld and Nicolson.*

Figueiró, H. V.; Li, G.; Trindade, F. J.; Assis, J.; and others. 2017. *Genome-wide signatures of complex introgression and adaptive evolution in the big cats. Science Advances, 3(7): e1700299.*

Ghezzo, E., and Rook, L. 2015. *The remarkable Panthera pardus (Felidae, Mammalia) record from Equi (Massa, Italy): taphonomy, morphology, and paleoecology. Quaternary Science Reviews, 110: 131-151.*

Hedges, L.; Lam, W. Y.; Campos-Arceiz, A.; Rayan, D. M.; and others. 2015. *Melanistic leopards reveal their spots: Infrared camera traps provide a population density estimate of leopards in Malaysia. Abstract only The Journal of Wildlife Management, 79(5): 846-853.*

Heptner, V. G., and Sludskii, A. A. 1972. *Mammals of the Soviet Union, volume II, part 2: Carnivora (hyaenas and cats). Moscow: Vysshaya Shkola Publishers. English translation by Rao, P., 1992. General editor: Kothekar, V. S. New Delhi: Amerind Publishing. https://archive.org/details/mammalsofsov221992gept*

Jacobson, A. P.; Gerngross, P.; Lemeris Jr, J. R.; Schoonover, R. F.; and others. 2016. *Leopard (Panthera pardus) status, distribution, and the research efforts across its range. PeerJ 4 : e1974.*

Johnson, W. E.; Eizirik, E.; Pecon-Slattery, J.; Murphy, W. J.; and others. 2006. *The Late Miocene radiation of modern Felidae: A genetic assessment. Science, 311: 73-77.*

Kawanishi, K.; Sunquist, M. E.; Eizirik, E.; Lynam, A. J.; and others. 2010. *Near fixation of melanism in leopards of the Malay Peninsula. Journal of Zoology, 282(3): 201-206.*

Kitchener, A. C.; Van Valkenburgh, B.; and Yamaguchi, N. 2010. *Felid form and function, in Biology and Conservation of Wild Felids, ed. Macdonald, D. W., and Loveridge, A. J., 83-106. Oxford: Oxford University Press.*

Kitchener, A. C.; Breitenmoser-Würsten, C.; Eizirik, E.; Gentry, A.; and others. 2017. *A revised taxonomy of the Felidae: The final report of the Cat Classification Task Force of the IUCN Cat Specialist Group. https://repository.si.edu/bitstream/handle/10088/32616/A_revised_Felidae_Taxonomy_CatNews.pdf*

Macdonald, D. W.; Loveridge, A. J.; and Nowell, K. 2010. *Dramatis personae: An introduction to the wild felids, in Biology and Conservation of Wild Felids, eds. Macdonald, D. W., and Loveridge, A. J., 3-58. Oxford: Oxford University Press.*

Nyakatura, K., and Bininda-Emonds, O. R. P. 2012. *Updating the evolutionary history of Carnivora (Mammalia): a new species-level supertree complete with divergence time estimates. BMC Biology, 10:12.*

O'Brien, S. J., and Johnson, W. E. 2005. *Big cat genomics. Annual Review of Genomics and Human Genetics,* 6: 407-429.

O'Brien, S. J., and Johnson, W. E. 2007. *The evolution of cats. Scientific American.* 297 (1): 68-75.

Odden, M.; Athreya, V.; Rattan, S.; and Linnell, J. D. 2014. *Adaptable neighbours: movement patterns of GPS-collared leopards in human dominated landscapes in India. PLoS One, 9(11): e112044.*

Seidensticker, J. 1976. *On the ecological separation between tigers and leopards. Biotropica: 225-234.*

da Silva, L. G. 2017. *Ecology and Evolution of Melanism in Big Cats: Case Study with Black Leopards and Jaguars, in Big Cats. IntechOpen. https://www.intechopen.com/books/big-cats/ecology-and-evolution-of-melanism-in-big-cats-case-study-with-black-leopards-and-jaguars*

Stein, A.B.; Athreya, V.; Gerngross, P.; Balme, G.; and others. 2016. *Panthera pardus (errata version published in 2016). The IUCN Red List of Threatened Species 2016: e.T15954A102421779. https://www.iucnredlist.org/species/15954/102421779*

Sunquist, M. and Sunquist, F. 2002. *Wild Cats of the World. Chicago and London: University of Chicago Press. Retrieved from https://play.google.com/store/books/details?id=IF8nDwAAQBAJ*

Turner, A., and Antón, M. 1997. *The Big Cats and Their Fossil Relatives: An Illustrated Guide to Their Evolution and Natural History. New York: Columbia University Press.*

Uphyrkina, O.; Johnson, W. E.; Quigley, H.; Miquelle, D.; and others. 2001. *Phylogenetics, genome diversity and origin of modern leopard, Panthera pardus. Molecular Ecology, 10(11): 2617-2633.*

Werdelin, L.; Yamaguchi, N.; Johnson, W. E.; and O'Brien, S. J. 2010. *Phylogeny and evolution of cats (Felidae), in Biology and Conservation of Wild Felids, eds. Macdonald, D. W., and Loveridge, A. J., 59-82. Oxford: Oxford University Press.*

Werdelin, L., and Dehghani, R. 2011. *Carnivora, in Paleontology and Geology of Laetoli: Human Evolution in Context, Volume 2: Fossil Hominins and the Associated Fauna, Harrison, T., ed., 189-232. Springer, Dordrecht.*

Wibisono, H. T.; Wahyudi, H. A.; Wilianto, E.; Pinondang, I. M. R.; and others. 2018. *Identifying priority conservation landscapes and actions for the Critically Endangered Javan leopard in Indonesia: Conserving the last large carnivore in Java Island. PloS one, 13(6): e0198369.*

Wikipedia. 2019. *Leopard. https://en.wikipedia.org/wiki/Leopard Last accessed August 13, 2019.*

Cat Specialist Group. 2019. *Jaguar*. *http://www.catsg.org/index.php?id=95* *Last accessed August 25, 2019.*

Cavalcanti, S. C.; Marchini, S.; Zimmermann, A.; Gese, E. M.; and Macdonald, D. W. 2010. *Jaguars, livestock, and people in Brazil: realities and perceptions behind the conflict, in Biology and Conservation of Wild Felids, eds. Macdonald, D. W., and Loveridge, A. J., 383-402. Oxford: Oxford University Press.*

Culver, M.; Driscoll, C.; Eizirik, E.; and Spong, G. 2010. *Genetic applications in wild felids, in Biology and Conservation of Wild Felids, ed. Macdonald, D. W., and Loveridge, A. J., 107-124. Oxford: Oxford University Press.*

Eizirik, E.; Kim, J. H.; Menotti-Raymond, M.; Crawshaw Jr, P. G.; and others. 2001. *Phylogeography, population history and conservation genetics of jaguars (Panthera onca, Mammalia, Felidae). Molecular Ecology, 10(1): 65-79.*

Eizirik, E.; Yuhki, N.; Johnson, W. E.; Menotti-Raymond, M.; Hannah, S. S.; and O'Brien, S. J. 2003. *Molecular genetics and evolution of melanism in the cat family. Current Biology. 13: 448-453.*

Figueiró, H. V.; Li, G.; Trindade, F. J.; Assis, J.; and others. 2017. *Genome-wide signatures of complex introgression and adaptive evolution in the big cats. Science Advances, 3(7): e1700299.*

Ewer, R. F. 1973. *The carnivores. The World Naturalist, ed. Carrington, R. London: Weidenfeld and Nicolson.*

Figueiró, H. V.; Li, G.; Trindade, F. J.; Assis, J.; and others. 2017. *Genome-wide signatures of complex introgression and adaptive evolution in the big cats. Science Advances, 3(7), e1700299.*

Johnson, W. E.; Eizirik, E.; Pecon-Slattery, J.; Murphy, W. J.; and others. 2006. *The Late Miocene radiation of modern Felidae: A genetic assessment. Science, 311:73-77.*

Kitchener, A. C.; Van Valkenburgh, B.; and Yamaguchi, N. 2010. *Felid form and function, in Biology and Conservation of Wild Felids, ed. Macdonald, D. W., and Loveridge, A. J., 83-106. Oxford: Oxford University Press.*

Kitchener, A. C.; Breitenmoser-Würsten, C.; Eizirik, E.; Gentry, A.; and others. 2017. *A revised taxonomy of the Felidae: The final report of the Cat Classification Task Force of the IUCN Cat Specialist Group. https://repository.si.edu/bitstream/handle/10088/32616/A_revised_Felidae_Taxonomy_CatNews.pdf*

Li, G.; Figueiró, H. V.; Eizirik, E.; and Murphy, W. J. 2019. *Recombination-aware phylogenomics reveals the structured genomic landscape of hybridizing cat species. Molecular Biology and Evolution. https://academic.oup.com/mbe/advance-article-pdf/doi/10.1093/molbev/msz139/28824386/msz139.pdf*

Martin, L. D., and Neuner, A. M. 1978. *The end of the Pleistocene in America. Transactions of the Nebraska Academy of Sciences and Affiliated Societies, 337. https://digitalcommons.unl.edu/cgi/viewcontent.cgi?article=1336&context=tnas Last accessed November 26, 2019.*

Macdonald, D. W.; Loveridge, A. J.; and Nowell, K. 2010. *Dramatis personae: An introduction to the wild felids, in Biology and Conservation of Wild Felids, eds. Macdonald, D. W., and Loveridge, A. J., 3-58. Oxford: Oxford University Press.*

Macdonald, D. W.; Loveridge, A. J.; and Rabinowitz, A. 2010a. *Felid futures: crossing disciplines, borders, and generations, in Biology and Conservation of Wild Felids, eds. Macdonald, D. W., and Loveridge, A. J., 599-649. Oxford: Oxford University Press.*

Moreno, A. K. M., and Lima-Ribeiro, M. S. 2015. *Ecological niche models, fossil record and the multi-temporal calibration for Panthera onca (Linnaeus, 1758)(Mammalia: Felidae). Brazilian Journal of Biological Sciences, 2(4): 309-319.*

Nyakatura, K., and Bininda-Emonds, O. R. P. 2012. *Updating the evolutionary history of Carnivora (Mammalia): a new species-level supertree complete with divergence time estimates. BMC Biology, 10:12.*

O'Brien, S. J., and Johnson, W. E. 2005. Big cat genomics. *Annual Review of Genomics and Human Genetics, 6*: 407-429.

O'Brien, S. J., and Johnson, W. E. 2007. The evolution of cats. *Scientific American, 297 (1)*: 68-75.

de Oliveira, T. G., and Pereira, J. A. 2014. Intraguild predation and interspecific killing as structuring forces of carnivoran communities in South America. *Journal of Mammalian Evolution, 21(4)*: 427-436.

Quigley, H.; Foster, R.; Petracca, L.; Payan, E.; and others. 2017. Panthera onca (errata version published in 2018). The IUCN Red List of Threatened Species 2017: e.T15953A123791436. https://www.iucnredlist.org/species/15953/123791436

San Diego Zoo. 2019. Jaguar: Panthera onca. https://animals.sandiegozoo.org/animals/jaguar Last accessed November 25, 2019.

Schultz, C. B.; Martin, L. D.; and Schultz, M. R. 1984. A Pleistocene jaguar from North-Central Nebraska. Transactions of the Nebraska Academy of Sciences and Affiliated Societies, 228. https://digitalcommons.unl.edu/cgi/viewcontent.cgi?article=1227&context=tnas Last accessed November 26, 2019.

Scognamillo, D.; Maxit, I. E.; Sunquist, M.; and Polisar, J. 2003. Coexistence of jaguar (Panthera onca) and puma (Puma concolor) in a mosaic landscape in the Venezuelan llanos. Journal of Zoology, 259(3): 269-279.

Smith, F. A.; Tomé, C. P.; Elliott Smith, E. A.; Lyons, S. K.; and others. 2016. Unraveling the consequences of the terminal Pleistocene megafauna extinction on mammal community assembly. Ecography, 39(2): 223-239.

Sunquist, M. and Sunquist, F. 2002. Wild Cats of the World. Chicago and London: University of Chicago Press. Retrieved from https://play.google.com/store/books/details?id=IF8nDwAAQBAJ

Thapa, K; Wikramanayake, E; Malla, S; Acharya, K. P.; and others. 2017 Tigers in the Terai: Strong evidence for meta-population dynamics contributing to tiger recovery and conservation in the Terai Arc Landscape. PLoS ONE 12(6): e0177548.

Turner, A., and Antón, M. 1997. The Big Cats and Their Fossil Relatives: An Illustrated Guide to Their Evolution and Natural History. New York: Columbia University Press.

Werdelin, L.; Yamaguchi, N.; Johnson, W. E.; and O'Brien, S. J. 2010. Phylogeny and evolution of cats (Felidae), in Biology and Conservation of Wild Felids, eds. Macdonald, D. W., and Loveridge, A. J., 59-82. Oxford: Oxford University Press.

Werdelin, L., and Dehghani, R. 2011. Carnivora, in Paleontology and Geology of Laetoli: Human Evolution in Context, Volume 2: Fossil Hominins and the Associated Fauna, Harrison, T., ed., 189-232. Springer, Dordrecht.

Wikipedia. 2019. Jaguar. Last accessed November 26, 2019.

___. 2019. Jaguars in Mesoamerican culture. https://en.wikipedia.org/wiki/Jaguars_in_Mesoamerican_cultures Last accessed August 28, 2019.

___. 2019. Panthera gombaszoegensis. https://en.wikipedia.org/wiki/Panthera_gombaszoegensis Last accessed November 15, 2019.

Cat Specialist Group. 2019. Snow leopard. http://www.catsg.org/index.php?id=100 Last accessed May 17, 2019.

Cho, Y. S.; Hu, L.; Hou, H.; Lee, H.; and others. 2013. The tiger genome and comparative analysis with lions and snow leopard genomes. Nature Communications, 4:24-33.

Christiansen, P. 2008. Phylogeny of the great cats (Felidae: Pantherinae), and the influence of fossil taxa and missing characters. Cladistics, 24(6): 977-992.

Ewer, R. F. 1973. The carnivores. The World Naturalist, ed. Carrington, R. London: Weidenfeld and Nicolson.

Gradstein, F. M.; Ogg, J. G.; and Hilgen, F. G. 2012. On the geologic time scale. Newsletters on Stratigraphy. 45(2): 171-188.

Heptner, V. G., and Sludskii, A. A. 1972. Mammals of the Soviet Union, volume II, part 2: Carnivora (hyaenas and cats). Moscow: Vysshaya Shkola Publishers. English translation by Rao, P., 1992. General editor: Kothekar, V. S. New Delhi: Amerind Publishing. https://archive.org/details/mammalsofsov221992gept

Jackson, R. M.; Mishra, C.; McCarthy, T. M.; and Ale, S. B. 2010. Snow leopards: conflict and conservation, in Biology and Conservation of Wild Felids, eds. Macdonald, D. W., and Loveridge, A. J., 417-430. Oxford: Oxford University Press.

Johnson, W. E.; Eizirik, E.; Pecon-Slattery, J.; Murphy, W. J.; and others. 2006. The Late Miocene radiation of modern Felidae: A genetic assessment. Science, 311:73-77.

Kitchener, A. C.; Van Valkenburgh, B.; and Yamaguchi, N. 2010. Felid form and function, in Biology and Conservation of Wild Felids, ed. Macdonald, D. W., and Loveridge, A. J., 83-106. Oxford: Oxford University Press.

Kitchener, A. C.; Breitenmoser-Würsten, C.; Eizirik, E.; Gentry, A.; and others. 2017. A revised taxonomy of the Felidae: The final report of the Cat Classification Task Force of the IUCN Cat Specialist Group. https://repository.si.edu/bitstream/handle/10088/32616/A_revised_Felidae_Taxonomy_CatNews.pdf

Macdonald, D. W.; Loveridge, A. J.; and Nowell, K. 2010. Dramatis personae: An introduction to the wild felids, in Biology and Conservation of Wild Felids, eds. Macdonald, D. W., and Loveridge, A. J., 3-58. Oxford: Oxford University Press.

McCarthy, T.; Mallon, D.; Jackson, R.; Zahler, P.; and McCarthy, K. 2017. Panthera uncia. The IUCN Red List of Threatened Species 2017: e.T22732A50664030. https://www.iucnredlist.org/species/22732/50664030

Nyakatura, K., and Bininda-Emonds, O. R. P. 2012. Updating the evolutionary history of Carnivora (Mammalia): a new species-level supertree complete with divergence time estimates. BMC Biology, 10:12.

O'Brien, S. J., and Johnson, W. E. 2007. The evolution of cats. Scientific American, 297 (1): 68-75.

Sunquist, M. and Sunquist, F. 2002. Wild Cats of the World. Chicago and London: University of Chicago Press. Retrieved from https://play.google.com/store/books/details?id=IF8nDwAAQBAJ

Tseng, Z. J.; Wang, X.; Slater, G. J.; Takeuchi, G. T.; and others. 2014. Himalayan fossils of the oldest known pantherine establish ancient origin of big cats. Proceedings of the Royal Society B: Biological Sciences, 281(1774): 20132686.

Turner, A., and Antón, M. 1997. The Big Cats and Their Fossil Relatives: An Illustrated Guide to Their Evolution and Natural History. New York: Columbia University Press.

Wang, J.; Laguardia, A.; Damerell, P. J.; Riordan, P.; and Shi, K. (2014). Dietary overlap of snow leopard and other carnivores in the Pamirs of Northwestern China. Chinese Science Bulletin, 59(25): 3162-3168.

Werdelin, L.; Yamaguchi, N.; Johnson, W. E.; and O'Brien, S. J. 2010. Phylogeny and evolution of cats (Felidae), in Biology and Conservation of Wild Felids, eds. Macdonald, D. W., and Loveridge, A. J., 59-82. Oxford: Oxford University Press.

Wikipedia. 2019. Snow leopard. https://en.wikipedia.org/wiki/Snow_leopard Last accessed May 17, 2019.

Allen, M. L.; Wittmer, H. U.; Setiawan, E.; Jaffe, S.; and Marshall, A. J. *2016. Scent marking in Sunda clouded leopards (Neofelis diardi): novel observations close a key gap in understanding felid communication behaviours. Scientific Reports, 6: 35433.*

Cat Specialist Group: Mainland and **Sunda clouded leopards**. *http://www.catsg.org/index.php?id=116 and http://www.catsg.org/index.php?id=225. Last accessed September 17, 2017.*

Christiansen, P. *2008. Evolutionary changes in craniomandibular shape in the great cats (Neofelis Griffith and Panthera Oken). Biological Journal of the Linnaean Society. 95:766-788.*

___. *2008a. Phylogeny of the great cats (Felidae: Pantherinae), and the influence of fossil taxa and missing characters. Cladistics, 24(6): 977-992.*

___. *2008b. Species distinction and evolutionary differences in the clouded leopard (Neofelis nebulosa) and Diard's clouded leopard (Neofelis diardi). Journal of Mammalogy, 89(6): 1435-1446.*

Culver, M.; Driscoll, C.; Eizirik, E.; and Spong, G. *2010. Genetic applications in wild felids, in Biology and Conservation of Wild Felids, ed. Macdonald, D. W. and Loveridge, A. J., 107-123. Oxford: Oxford University Press, Oxford.*

Ewer, R. F. *1973. The carnivores. The World Naturalist, ed. Carrington, R. London: Weidenfeld and Nicolson.*

Grassman, L.; Lynam, A.; Mohamad, S.; Duckworth, J.W.; and others. *2016. Neofelis nebulosa. The IUCN Red List of Threatened Species 2016: e.T14519A97215090. https://www.iucnredlist.org/species/14519/97215090 Last accessed September 24, 2019.*

Haidir, I. A.; Dinata, Y.; Linkie, M.; and Macdonald, D. W. *2013. Asiatic golden cat and Sunda clouded leopard occupancy in the Kerinci Seblat landscape, West-Central Sumatra. Cat News, 59: 7-10.*

Hearn, A.; Ross, J.; Brodie, J.; Cheyne, S.; and others. *2015. Neofelis diardi (errata version published in 2016). The IUCN Red List of Threatened Species 2015: e.T136603A97212874 https://www.iucnredlist.org/species/136603/97212874*

Heptner, V. G., and Sludskii, A. A. *1972. Mammals of the Soviet Union, volume II, part 2: Carnivora (hyaenas and cats). Moscow: Vysshaya Shkola Publishers. English translation by Rao, P., 1992. General editor: Kothekar, V. S. New Delhi: Amerind Publishing. https://archive.org/details/mammalsofsov221992gept*

Johnson, W. E.; Eizirik, E.; Pecon-Slattery, J.; Murphy, W. J.; and others. *2006. The Late Miocene Radiation of Modern Felidae: A Genetic Assessment. Science, 311:73-77.*

Kitchener, A. C.; Van Valkenburgh, B.; and Yamaguchi, N. *2010. Felid form and function, in Biology and Conservation of Wild Felids, ed. Macdonald, D. W., and Loveridge, A. J., 83-106. Oxford: Oxford University Press.*

Kitchener, A. C.; Breitenmoser-Würsten, C.; Eizirik, E.; Gentry, A.; and others. *2017. A revised taxonomy of the Felidae: The final report of the Cat Classification Task Force of the IUCN Cat Specialist Group. https://repository.si.edu/bitstream/handle/10088/32616/A_revised_Felidae_Taxonomy_CatNews.pdf*

Lee, S. *2017. Move to protect the Sunda clouded leopard. The Star. http://www.thestar.com.my/news/nation/2017/06/12/move-to-protect-the-sunda-clouded-leopard/#iQuVGjP6h94qzKT2.01 Last accessed September 17, 2017.*

Macdonald, D. W.; Loveridge, A. J.; and Nowell, K. *2010. Dramatis personae: an introduction to the wild felids, in Biology and Conservation of Wild Felids, ed. Macdonald, D. W. and Loveridge, A. J., 3-58. Oxford: Oxford University Press, Oxford.*

Nyakatura, K., and Bininda-Emonds, O. R. P. 2012. Updating the evolutionary history of Carnivora (Mammalia): a new species-level supertree complete with divergence time estimates. BMC Biology. 10:12.

O'Brien, S. J., and Johnson, W. E. 2007. The evolution of cats. Scientific American. 297 (1):68-75.

de Queiroz, K. 2007. Species concepts and species delimitation. Systematic Biology, 56(6): 879-886.

Ridout, M. S., and Linkie, M. 2009. Estimating overlap of daily activity patterns from camera trap data. Journal of Agricultural, Biological, and Environmental Statistics, 14(3): 322-337.

Sunquist, M. and Sunquist, F. 2002. Wild Cats of the World. Chicago and London: University of Chicago Press. Retrieved from https://play.google.com/store/books/details?id=IF8nDwAAQBAJ

Tan, C. K. W.; Rocha, D. G.; Clements, G. R.; Brenes-Mora, E.; and others. 2017. Habitat use and predicted range for the mainland clouded leopard Neofelis nebulosa in Peninsular Malaysia. Biological Conservation, 206: 65-74.

Werdelin, L., and Olsson, L. 1997. How the leopard got its spots: a phylogenetic view off the evolution of felid coat patterns. Biological Journal of the Linnaen Society. 62:383-400.

Werdelin, L.; Yamaguchi, N.; Johnson, W. E.; and O'Brien, S. J.. 2010. Phylogeny and evolution of cats (Felidae), in Biology and Conservation of Wild Felids, eds. Macdonald, D. W., and Loveridge, A. J., 59-82. Oxford: Oxford University Press.

Wikipedia. 2019. **Mainland** and **Sunda clouded leopards**. https://en.wikipedia.org/wiki/Clouded_leopard and https://en.wikipedia.org/wiki/Sunda_clouded_leopard Last accessed September 24, 2019.

Wilting, A.; Christiansen, P.; Kitchener, A. C.; Kemp, Y. J. M.; and others. 2011. Geographical variation in and evolutionary history of the Sunda clouded leopard (Neofelis diardi) (Mammalia: Carnivora: Felidae) with the description of a new subspecies from Borneo. Molecular Phylogenetics and Evolution, 58: 317-328.

Beier, P. *1991. Cougar attacks on humans in the United States and Canada. Wildlife Society Bulletin, 19(4): 403-412.*

Caragiulo, A.; Dias-Freedman, I.; Clark, J. A.; Rabinowitz, S.; and Amato, G. *2014. Mitochondrial DNA sequence variation and phylogeography of Neotropic pumas (Puma concolor). Mitochondrial DNA, 25(4): 304-312.*

Cat Specialist Group. *2020. Puma. http://www.catsg.org/index.php?id=94 Last accessed January 29, 2020.*

Chimento, N. R., and Dondas, A. *2018. First record of Puma concolor (Mammalia, Felidae) in the early-middle pleistocene of South America. Journal of Mammalian Evolution, 25(3); 381-389.*

Cougar Network. *2015. https://www.cougarnet.org/*

Culver, M.; Johnson, W. E.; Pecon-Slattery, J.; and O'Brien, S. J. *2000. Genomic ancestry of the American puma (Puma concolor). Journal of Heredity, 91(3): 186-197.*

Eizirik, E.; Yuhki, N.; Johnson, W. E.; Menotti-Raymond, M.; Hannah, S. S.; and O'Brien, S. J. *2003. Molecular genetics and evolution of melanism in the cat family. Current Biology, 13: 448-453.*

Ewer, R. F. *1973. The carnivores. The World Naturalist, ed. Carrington, R. London: Weidenfeld and Nicolson.*

Glick, H. B. *2014. Modeling cougar habitat in the Northeastern United States. Ecological Modelling, 285: 78-89.*

Johnson, W. E.; Eizirik, E.; Pecon-Slattery, J.; Murphy, W. J.; and others. *2006. The Late Miocene Radiation of Modern Felidae: A Genetic Assessment. Science, 311:73-77.*

Kitchener, A. C.; Breitenmoser-Würsten, C.; Eizirik, E.; Gentry, A.; and others. *2017. A revised taxonomy of the Felidae: The final report of the Cat Classification Task Force of the IUCN Cat Specialist Group. https://repository.si.edu/bitstream/handle/10088/32616/A_revised_Felidae_Taxonomy_CatNews.pdf*

LaRue, M. A., and Nielsen, C. K. *2016. Population viability of recolonizing cougars in midwestern North America. Ecological Modelling, 321: 121-129.*

Loveridge, A.; Wang, S. W.; Frank, L.; and Seidensticker, J. *2010. People and wild felids: conservation of cats and management of conflicts, in Biology and Conservation of Wild Felids, eds. Macdonald, D. W., and Loveridge, A. J., 161-195. Oxford: Oxford University Press.*

Macdonald, D. W.; Loveridge, A. J.; and Nowell, K. *2010. Dramatis personae: An introduction to the wild felids, in Biology and Conservation of Wild Felids, eds. Macdonald, D. W., and Loveridge, A. J., 3-58. Oxford: Oxford University Press.*

Maser, C. *1998. Mammals of the Pacific Northwest. Corvallis: Oregon State University Press.*

Matte, E. M.; Castilho, C. S.; Miotto, R. A.; Sana, D. A.; and others. *2013. Molecular evidence for a recent demographic expansion in the puma (Puma concolor)(Mammalia, Felidae). Genetics and Molecular Biology, 36(4): 586-597.*

Mattson, D.; Logan, K.; and Sweanor, L. *2011. Factors governing risk of cougar attacks on humans. Human-Wildlife Interactions, 5(1): 135-158.*

McKee, D. *2003. Cougar attacks on humans: a case report. Wilderness and Environmental Medicine, 14(3): 169-173.*

Murphy, T., and Macdonald, D. W. *(2010). Pumas and people: lessons in the landscape of tolerance from a widely distributed felid, in Biology and Conservation of Wild Felids, eds. Macdonald, D. W., and Loveridge, A. J., 431-451. Oxford: Oxford University Press.*

Nielsen, C.; Thompson, D.; Kelly, M.; and Lopez-Gonzalez, C.A. 2015. *Puma concolor (errata version published in 2016). The IUCN Red List of Threatened Species 2015: e.T18868A97216466. https://www.iucnredlist.org/species/18868/97216466*

New Mexico Department of Game and Fish. *n. d. Cougar Education and Identification Course. http://www.wildlife.state.nm.us/download/hunting/species/cougar/course/Cougar-Education-Booklet-1-31-11.pdf Last accessed March 16, 2019.*

Nielsen, C.; Thompson, D.; Kelly, M.; and Lopez-Gonzalez, C.A. 2015. *Puma concolor. The IUCN Red List of Threatened Species 2015: e.T18868A97216466.*

O'Brien, S. J., and Johnson, W. E. 2007. *The evolution of cats. Scientific American. 297 (1):68-75.*

de Oliveira, T. G., and Pereira, J. A. 2014. *Intraguild predation and interspecific killing as structuring forces of carnivoran communities in South America. Journal of Mammalian Evolution, 21(4): 427-436.*

San Diego Zoo. 2019. *Mountain lion. https://animals.sandiegozoo.org/animals/mountain-lion-puma-cougar Last accessed March 16, 2019.*

Scognamillo, D.; Maxit, I. E.; Sunquist, M.; and Polisar, J. 2003. *Coexistence of jaguar (Panthera onca) and puma (Puma concolor) in a mosaic landscape in the Venezuelan llanos. Journal of Zoology, 259(3): 269-279.*

Van Valkenburgh, B. 1989. *Carnivore dental adaptations and diet: A study of trophic diversity within guilds, in Carnivore Behavior, Ecology, and Evolution, ed. J. L., Gittleman, Volume 1, 410-436. Ithaca, NY: Cornell University Press.*

Wikipedia. 2020. *Cougar. https://en.wikipedia.org/wiki/Cougar Last accessed January 29, 2020.*

Caso, A. 2013. *Spatial differences and local avoidance of Ocelot (Leopardus pardalis) and Jaguarundi (Puma yagouaroundi) in northeast Mexico. Texas A&M University-Kingsville.*

Caso, A.; de Oliveira, T.; and Carvajal, S.V. 2015. *Herpailurus yagouaroundi. The IUCN Red List of Threatened Species 2015: e.T9948A50653167. https://www.iucnredlist.org/species/9948/50653167*

Cat Specialist Group. 2019. *Jaguarundi. http://www.catsg.org/index.php?id=93 Last accessed September 23, 2019.*

Eizirik, E.; Yuhki, N.; Johnson, W. E.; Menotti-Raymond, M.; and others. 2003. *Molecular genetics and evolution of melanism in the cat family. Current Biology. 13: 448-453.*

Ewer, R. F. 1973. *The carnivores. The World Naturalist, ed. Carrington, R. London: Weidenfeld and Nicolson.*

Giordano, A. J. 2016. *Ecology and status of the jaguarundi P uma yagouaroundi: a synthesis of existing knowledge. Mammal Review, 46(1): 30-43.*

Johnson, G. 2019. *Jaguarundi. https://www.outdooralabama.com/carnivores/jaguarundi Last accessed September 26, 2019.*

Johnson, W. E.; Eizirik, E.; Pecon-Slattery, J.; Murphy, W. J.; and others. 2006. *The Late Miocene Radiation of Modern Felidae: A Genetic Assessment. Science, 311:73-77.*

Kitchener, A. C.; Breitenmoser-Würsten, C.; Eizirik, E.; Gentry, A.; and others. 2017. *A revised taxonomy of the Felidae: The final report of the Cat Classification Task Force of the IUCN Cat Specialist Group. https://repository.si.edu/bitstream/handle/10088/32616/A_revised_Felidae_Taxonomy_CatNews.pdf*

Macdonald, D. W.; Loveridge, A. J.; and Nowell, K. 2010. *Dramatis personae: An introduction to the wild felids, in Biology and Conservation of Wild Felids, eds. Macdonald, D. W., and Loveridge, A. J., 3-58. Oxford: Oxford University Press.*

Maffei, L.; Noss, A.; and Fiorello, C. 2007. *The jaguarundi (puma yagouaroundi) In the kaa iya del gran chaco national park, Santa Cruz, Bolivia. Mastozoología Neotropical, 14(2), 263-266. https://www.redalyc.org/pdf/457/45714211.pdf*

Migliorini, R. P.; Peters, F. B.; Favarini, M. O.; and Kasper, C. B. 2018. *Trophic ecology of sympatric small cats in the Brazilian Pampa. PloS One, 13(7): e0201257. https://journals.plos.org/plosone/article?id=10.1371/journal.pone.0201257*

O'Brien, S. J., and Johnson, W. E. 2007. *The evolution of cats. Scientific American. 297 (1):68-75.*

de Oliveira, T. G.; Tortato, M. A.; Silveira, L.; Kasper, C. B.; and others. 2010. *Ocelot ecology and its effect on the small-felid guild in the lowland neotropics, in Biology and Conservation of Wild Felids, ed. Macdonald, D. W., and Loveridge, A. J., 559-580. Oxford: Oxford University Press.*

Segura, V.; Prevosti, F.; and Cassini, G. 2013. *Cranial ontogeny in the Puma lineage, Puma concolor, Herpailurus yagouaroundi, and Acinonyx jubatus (Carnivora: Felidae): a three-dimensional geometric morphometric approach. Zoological Journal of the Linnean Society, 169(1): 235-250.*

Shostell, J. M., and Ruiz-Garcia, M. 2013. *An introduction to neotropical carnivores, in Molecular population genetics, evolutionary biology and biological conservation of the Neotropical carnivores. p, 1-36.*

Sunquist, M. and Sunquist, F. 2002. *Wild Cats of the World. Chicago and London: University of Chicago Press. Retrieved from https://play.google.com/store/books/details?id=IF8nDwAAQBAJ*

Werdelin, L.; Yamaguchi, N.; Johnson, W. E.; and O'Brien, S. J. 2010. *Phylogeny and evolution of cats (Felidae), in Biology and Conservation of Wild Felids, eds. Macdonald, D. W., and Loveridge, A. J., 59-82. Oxford: Oxford University Press.*

Wikipedia. 2019. *Jaguarundi. https://en.wikipedia.org/wiki/Jaguarundi Last accessed September 23, 2019.*

Cat Specialist Group. 2019. Cheetah. http://www.catsg.org/index.php?id=107 Last accessed September 29, 2019.

Charruau, P.; Fernandes, C.; Orozco-Terwengel, P.; Peters, J.; and others . 2011. Phylogeography, genetic structure and population divergence time of cheetahs in Africa and Asia: evidence for long-term geographic isolates. Molecular Ecology, 20(4): 706-724.

Culver, M.; Driscoll, C.; Eizirik, E.; and Spong, G. 2010. Genetic applications in wild felids, in Biology and Conservation of Wild Felids, ed. Macdonald, D. W., and Loveridge, A. J., 107-124. Oxford: Oxford University Press.

Dobrynin, P.; Liu, S.; Tamazian, G.; Xiong, Z.; and others. 2015. Genomic legacy of the African cheetah, Acinonyx jubatus. Genome Biology, 16(1): 277.

Durant, S. M. 2000. Predator avoidance, breeding experience and reproductive success in endangered cheetahs, Acinonyx jubatus. Animal Behaviour, 60(1): 121-130.

Durant, S. M.; Dickman, A. J.; Maddox, T.; Waweru, M. N.; and others. 2010. Past, present, and future of cheetahs in Tanzania: their behavioural ecology and conservation, in Biology and Conservation of Wild Felids, eds. Macdonald, D. W., and Loveridge, A. J., 373-382. Oxford: Oxford University Press.

Durant, S.; Mitchell, N.; Ipavec, A.; and Groom, R. 2015. Acinonyx jubatus. The IUCN Red List of Threatened Species 2015: e.T219A50649567 https://www.iucnredlist.org/species/219/50649567

Eklund, R.; Peters, G.; and Duthie, E. D. 2010. An acoustic analysis of purring in the cheetah (Acinonyx jubatus) and in the domestic cat (Felis catus), in Fonetik 2010, Lund University, 2– 4 June 2010, Lund, Sweden (pp. 17-22). Mediatryck.

Ewer, R. F. 1973. The carnivores. The World Naturalist, ed. Carrington, R. London: Weidenfeld and Nicolson.

Faurby, S., Werdelin, L., and Svenning, J. C. 2016. The difference between trivial and scientific names: There were never any true cheetahs in North America. Genome Biology. 17: 89.

Hayward, M. W.; Hofmeyr, M.; O'Brien, J.; and Kerley, G. I. H. 2006. Prey preferences of the cheetah (Acinonyx jubatus)(Felidae: Carnivora): morphological limitations or the need to capture rapidly consumable prey before kleptoparasites arrive?. Journal of Zoology, 270(4): 615-627.

Heptner, V. G., and Sludskii, A. A. 1972. Mammals of the Soviet Union, volume II, part 2: Carnivora (hyaenas and cats). Moscow: Vysshaya Shkola Publishers. English translation by Rao, P., 1992. General editor: Kothekar, V. S. New Delhi: Amerind Publishing. https://archive.org/details/mammalsofsov221992gept

Herbst, M. 2009. Behavioural ecology and population genetics of the African wild cat, Felis silvestris Forster 1870, in the southern Kalahari. PhD thesis, University of Pretoria.

Hudson, P. E.; Corr, S. A.; Payne-Davis, R. C.; Clancy, S. N.; and others. 2010. Functional anatomy of the cheetah (Acinonyx jubatus) hindlimb. Journal of anatomy, 218(4): 363-374.

Hudson, P. E.; Corr, S. A.; Payne-Davis, R. C.; Clancy, S. N.; and others. 2011. Functional anatomy of the cheetah (Acinonyx jubatus) forelimb. Journal of Anatomy, 218(4): 375-385.

Johnson, W. E.; Eizirik, E.; Pecon-Slattery, J.; Murphy, W. J.; and others. 2006. The Late Miocene Radiation of Modern Felidae: A Genetic Assessment. Science, 311:73-77.

Kelly, M. J.; Laurenson, M. K.; FitzGibbon, C. D.; Collins, D. A.; and others. 1998. Demography of the Serengeti cheetah (Acinonyx jubatus) population: the first 25 years. Journal of Zoology, 244(4): 473-488.

Kitchener, A. C.; Van Valkenburgh, B.; and Yamaguchi, N. 2010. Felid form and function, in Biology and Conservation of Wild Felids, ed. Macdonald, D. W., and Loveridge, A. J., 83-106. Oxford: Oxford University Press.

Kitchener, A. C.; Breitenmoser-Würsten, C.; Eizirik, E.; Gentry, A.; and others. 2017. *A revised taxonomy of the Felidae: The final report of the Cat Classification Task Force of the IUCN Cat Specialist Group. https://repository.si.edu/bitstream/handle/10088/32616/A_revised_Felidae_Taxonomy_CatNews.pdf*

Krausman, P. R., and Morales, S. M. 2005. *Acinonyx jubatus. Mammalian Species, 2005(771): 1-6. https://academic.oup.com/mspecies/article-pdf/doi/10.1644/771/8071728/771-1.pdf*

Londei, T. 2000. *The cheetah (Acinonyx jubatus) dewclaw: specialization overlooked. Journal of Zoology, 251(4): 535-547. (Abstract only)*

Loveridge, A.; Wang, S. W.; Frank, L.; and Seidensticker, J. 2010. *People and wild felids: conservation of cats and management of conflicts, in Biology and Conservation of Wild Felids, eds. Macdonald, D. W., and Loveridge, A. J., 161-195. Oxford: Oxford University Press.*

Macdonald, D. W.; Loveridge, A. J.; and Nowell, K. 2010. *Dramatis personae: An introduction to the wild felids, in Biology and Conservation of Wild Felids, eds. Macdonald, D. W., and Loveridge, A. J., 3-58. Oxford: Oxford University Press.*

Macdonald, D. W;, Mosser, A.; and Gittleman, J. L. 2010a. *Felid society, in Biology and Conservation of Wild Felids, eds. Macdonald, D. W., and Loveridge, A. J., 125-160. Oxford: Oxford University Press.*

Macdonald, D. W.; Loveridge, A. J.; and Rabinowitz, A. 2010b. *Felid futures: crossing disciplines, borders, and generations, in Biology and Conservation of Wild Felids, eds. Macdonald, D. W., and Loveridge, A. J., 599. Oxford: Oxford University Press.*

Marker, L.; Dickman, A. J.; Mills, M. G. L.; and Macdonald, D. W. 2010. *Cheetahs and ranchers in Namibia: a case study, in Biology and Conservation of Wild Felids, eds. Macdonald, D. W., and Loveridge, A. J., 353-372. Oxford: Oxford University Press.*

Nyakatura, K., and Bininda-Emonds, O. R. P. 2012. *Updating the evolutionary history of Carnivora (Mammalia): a new species-level supertree complete with divergence time estimates. BMC Biology, 10:12.*

O'Brien, S. J., and Johnson, W. E. 2007. *The evolution of cats. Scientific American. 297 (1):68-75.*

O'Brien, S. J.; Koepfli, K. P.; Eizirik, E.; Johnson, W.; and others. 2016. *Response to comment by Faurby, Werdelin and Svenning. Genome Biology. 17: 90.*

O' Brien, S. J.; Johnson, W. E.; Driscoll, C. A.; Dobrynin, P.; and Marker, L. 2017. *Conservation genetics of the cheetah: Lessons learned and new opportunities. Journal of Heredity, 108(6): 671-677.*

Turner, A., and Antón, M. 1997. *The Big Cats and Their Fossil Relatives: An Illustrated Guide to Their Evolution and Natural History. New York: Columbia University Press.*

Van Valkenburgh, B. 1989. *Carnivore dental adaptations and diet: A study of trophic diversity within guilds, in Carnivore Behavior, Ecology, and Evolution, Vol. 1., ed. Gittleman, J. L., 410-436. Ithaca, NY: Cornell University Press.*

Werdelin, L., and Dehghani, R. 2011. *Carnivora, in Paleontology and Geology of Laetoli: Human Evolution in Context, Volume 2: Fossil Hominins and the Associated Fauna, Harrison, T., ed., 189-232. Springer, Dordrecht.*

Werdelin, L.; Yamaguchi, N.; Johnson, W. E.; and O'Brien, S. J. 2010. *Phylogeny and evolution of cats (Felidae), in Biology and Conservation of Wild Felids, eds. Macdonald, D. W., and Loveridge, A. J., 59-82. Oxford: Oxford University Press.*

Wikipedia. 2019. *Cheetah. https://en.wikipedia.org/wiki/Cheetah Last accessed September 29, 2019.*

Cat Specialist Group. 2020. Bobcat. *http://www.catsg.org/index.php?id=96* Last accessed January 7, 2020.

Chamberlain, M. J.; Leopold, B. D.; and Conner, L. M. 2003. Space use, movements and habitat selection of adult bobcats (Lynx rufus) in central Mississippi. The American Midland Naturalist, 149(2): 395-406.

Ewer, R. F. 1973. The carnivores. The World Naturalist, ed. Carrington, R. London: Weidenfeld and Nicolson.

Gradstein, F. M.; Ogg, J. G.; and Hilgen, F. G. 2012. On the geologic time scale. Newsletters on Stratigraphy, 45(2): 171-188.

Johnson, W. E.; Eizirik, E.; Pecon-Slattery, J.; Murphy, W. J.; and others. 2006. The Late Miocene Radiation of Modern Felidae: A Genetic Assessment. Science, 311:73-77.

Kelly, M.; Morin, D.; and Lopez-Gonzalez, C.A. 2016. Lynx rufus. The IUCN Red List of Threatened Species 2016: e.T12521A50655874 *https://www.iucnredlist.org/species/12521/50655874*

Kitchener, A. C.; Breitenmoser-Würsten, C.; Eizirik, E.; Gentry, A.; and others. 2017. A revised taxonomy of the Felidae: The final report of the Cat Classification Task Force of the IUCN Cat Specialist Group. *https://repository.si.edu/bitstream/handle/10088/32616/A_revised_Felidae_Taxonomy_CatNews.pdf*

Li, G.; Davis, B. W.; Eizirik, E.; and Murphy, W. J. 2016. Phylogenomic evidence for ancient hybridization in the genomes of living cats (Felidae). Genome Research, 26(1): 1-11.

Macdonald, D. W.; Loveridge, A. J.; and Nowell, K. 2010. "Dramatis personae": An introduction to the wild felids, in Biology and Conservation of Wild Felids, eds. Macdonald, D. W., and Loveridge, A. J., 3-58. Oxford: Oxford University Press.

Macdonald, D. W.; Yamaguchi, N.; Kitchener, A. C.; Daniels, M.; and others. 2010a. Reversing cryptic extinction: the history, present, and future of the Scottish wildcat, in Biology and Conservation of Wild Felids, ed. Macdonald, D. W., and Loveridge, A. J., 471-491. Oxford: Oxford University Press.

Major, J. T., and Sherburne, J. A. 1987. Interspecific relationships of coyotes, bobcats, and red foxes in western Maine. The Journal of Wildlife Management: 606-616. (Abstract only)

McCord, C. M. 1974. Selection of winter habitat by bobcats (Lynx rufus) on the Quabbin Reservation, Massachusetts. Journal of Mammalogy, 55(2): 428-437.

O'Brien, S. J., and Johnson, W. E. 2007. The evolution of cats. Scientific American. 297 (1):68-75.

de Oliveira, T. G.; Tortato, M. A.; Silveira, L.; Kasper, C. B.; and others. 2010. Ocelot ecology and its effect on the small-felid guild in the lowland neotropics, in Biology and Conservation of Wild Felids, ed. Macdonald, D. W., and Loveridge, A. J., 559-580. Oxford: Oxford University Press.

Sánchez-Cordero, V.; Stockwell, D.; Sarkar, S.; Liu, H.; and others. 2008. Competitive interactions between felid species may limit the southern distribution of bobcats Lynx rufus. Ecography, 31(6): 757-764.

Van Valkenburgh, B. 1989. Carnivore dental adaptations and diet: A study of trophic diversity within guilds, in Carnivore Behavior, Ecology, and Evolution, Vol. 1., ed. Gittleman, J. L., 410-436. Ithaca, NY: Cornell University Press.

Werdelin, L.; Yamaguchi, N.; Johnson, W. E.; and O'Brien, S. J. 2010. Phylogeny and evolution of cats (Felidae), in Biology and Conservation of Wild Felids, eds. Macdonald, D. W., and Loveridge, A. J., 59-82. Oxford: Oxford University Press.

Wikipedia. 2020. Bobcat. *https://en.wikipedia.org/wiki/Bobcat* Last accessed January 7, 2020.

Allen, W. L.; Cuthill, I. C.; Scott-Samuel, N. E.; and Baddeley, R. 2010. *Why the leopard got its spots: relating pattern development to ecology in felids. Proceedings of the Royal Society B: Biological Sciences, 278(1710): 1373-1380.*

Cat Specialist Group. 2020. *Canada lynx. http://www.catsg.org/index.php?id=97 Last accessed January 7, 2020.*

Johnson, W. E.; Eizirik, E.; Pecon-Slattery, J.; Murphy, W. J.; and others. 2006. *The Late Miocene Radiation of Modern Felidae: A Genetic Assessment. Science, 311:73-77.*

Kitchener, A. C.; Van Valkenburgh, B.; and Yamaguchi, N. 2010. *Felid form and function, in Biology and Conservation of Wild Felids, ed. Macdonald, D. W., and Loveridge, A. J., 83-106. Oxford: Oxford University Press.*

Kitchener, A. C.; Breitenmoser-Würsten, C.; Eizirik, E.; Gentry, A.; and others. 2017. *A revised taxonomy of the Felidae: The final report of the Cat Classification Task Force of the IUCN Cat Specialist Group. https://repository.si.edu/bitstream/handle/10088/32616/A_revised_Felidae_Taxonomy_CatNews.pdf*

Li, G.; Davis, B. W.; Eizirik, E.; and Murphy, W. J. 2016. *Phylogenomic evidence for ancient hybridization in the genomes of living cats (Felidae). Genome Research, 26(1): 1-11.*

Loveridge, A.; Wang, S. W.; Frank, L.; and Seidensticker, J. 2010. *People and wild felids: conservation of cats and management of conflicts, in Biology and Conservation of Wild Felids, eds. Macdonald, D. W., and Loveridge, A. J., 161-195. Oxford: Oxford University Press.*

Macdonald, D. W.; Loveridge, A. J.; and Nowell, K. 2010b. *"Dramatis personae": An introduction to the wild felids, in Biology and Conservation of Wild Felids, eds. Macdonald, D. W., and Loveridge, A. J., 3-58. Oxford: Oxford University Press.*

O'Brien, S. J., and Johnson, W. E. 2007. *The evolution of cats. Scientific American. 297 (1):68-75.*

O' Donoghue, M.; Slough, B. G.; Poole, K. G.; Boutin, S.; and others. (2010). *Cyclical dynamics and behaviour of Canada lynx in northern Canada, in Biology and Conservation of Wild Felids, eds. Macdonald, D. W., and Loveridge, A. J., 521-536. Oxford: Oxford University Press.*

Poole, K. G. 2003. *A review of the Canada lynx, Lynx canadensis, in Canada. The Canadian Field-Naturalist, 117(3): 360-376.*

Schwartz, M. K.; Pilgrim, K. L.; McKelvey, K. S.; Lindquist, E. L.; and others. 2004. *Hybridization between Canada lynx and bobcats: genetic results and management implications. Conservation Genetics, 5(3): 349-355.*

Van Valkenburgh, B. 1989. *Carnivore dental adaptations and diet: A study of trophic diversity within guilds, in Carnivore Behavior, Ecology, and Evolution, Volume 1, ed. Gittleman, J. L., 410-436. Ithaca, NY: Cornell University Press.*

Vashon, J. 2016. *Lynx canadensis. The IUCN Red List of Threatened Species 2016: e.T12518A101138963 https://www.iucnredlist.org/species/12518/101138963*

Werdelin, L.; Yamaguchi, N.; Johnson, W. E.; and O'Brien, S. J. 2010. *Phylogeny and evolution of cats (Felidae), in Biology and Conservation of Wild Felids, eds. Macdonald, D. W., and Loveridge, A. J., 59-82. Oxford: Oxford University Press.*

Wikipedia. 2020. *https://en.wikipedia.org/wiki/Canada_lynx Last accessed January 7, 2020.*

Breitenmoser, U.; Breitenmoser-Würsten, C.; Okarma, H.; Kaphegyi, T.; and others. 2000. Action plan for the conservation of the Eurasian lynx in Europe (Lynx lynx) (No. 18-112). Council of Europe.

Breitenmoser, U.; Breitenmoser-Würsten, C.; Lanz, T.; von Arx, M.; and others. 2015. Lynx lynx (errata version published in 2017). The IUCN Red List of Threatened Species 2015: e.T12519A121707666 https://www.iucnredlist.org/species/12519/121707666 Last accessed January 7, 2020.

Cat Specialist Group. 2020. http://www.catsg.org/index.php?id=99 Last accessed January 7, 2020.

Ewer, R. F.. 1973. The carnivores. The World Naturalist, ed. Carrington, R. London: Weidenfeld and Nicolson.

Heptner, V. G., and Sludskii, A. A. 1972. Mammals of the Soviet Union, volume II, part 2: Carnivora (hyaenas and cats). Moscow: Vysshaya Shkola Publishers. English translation by Rao, P., 1992. General editor: Kothekar, V. S. New Delhi: Amerind Publishing. https://archive.org/details/mammalsofsov221992gept

Hetherington, D. A.; Lord, T. C.; and Jacobi, R. M. 2006. New evidence for the occurrence of Eurasian lynx (Lynx lynx) in medieval Britain. Journal of Quaternary Science: Published for the Quaternary Research Association, 21(1): 3-8.

Johnson, W. E.; Eizirik, E.; Pecon-Slattery, J.; Murphy, W. J.; and others. 2006. The Late Miocene Radiation of Modern Felidae: A Genetic Assessment. Science, 311:73-77.

Kitchener, A. C.; Breitenmoser-Würsten, C.; Eizirik, E.; Gentry, A.; and others. 2017. A revised taxonomy of the Felidae: The final report of the Cat Classification Task Force of the IUCN Cat Specialist Group. https://repository.si.edu/bitstream/handle/10088/32616/A_revised_Felidae_Taxonomy_CatNews.pdf

Macdonald, D. W.; Loveridge, A. J.; and Nowell, K. 2010b. "Dramatis personae": An introduction to the wild felids, in Biology and Conservation of Wild Felids, eds. Macdonald, D. W., and Loveridge, A. J., 3-58. Oxford: Oxford University Press.

O'Brien, S. J., and Johnson, W. E. 2007. The evolution of cats. Scientific American. 297 (1):68-75.

Rueness, E. K.; Naidenko, S.; Trosvik, P.; and Stenseth, N. C. 2014. Large-scale genetic structuring of a widely distributed carnivore-the Eurasian lynx (Lynx lynx). PloS One, 9(4). https://journals.plos.org/plosone/article/file?type=printable&id=10.1371/journal.pone.0093675

van Dijk, J.; Andersen, T.; May, R.; Andersen, R.; and others. 2008. Foraging strategies of wolverines within a predator guild. Canadian Journal of Zoology, 86(9): 966-975.

von Arx, M. 2018. Lynx lynx . The IUCN Red List of Threatened Species 2018: e.T12519A134346234 https://www.iucnredlist.org/species/12519/134346234 Last accessed January 7, 2020.

Abascal, F.; Corvelo, A.; Cruz, F.; Villanueva-Cañas, J. L.; and others. 2016. *Extreme genomic erosion after recurrent demographic bottlenecks in the highly endangered Iberian lynx. Genome Biology, 17(1): 1-19.*

Allen, W. L.; Cuthill, I. C.; Scott-Samuel, N. E.; and Baddeley, R. 2011. *Why the leopard got its spots: relating pattern development to ecology in felids. Proceedings of the Royal Society B, 278: 1373-1380.*

Cat Specialist Group. 2020. *Iberian lynx. http://www.catsg.org/index.php?id=98 Last accessed January 7, 2020.*

Delibes, M.; Rodríguez, A.; and Ferreras, P. 2000. *Action plan for the conservation of the Iberian lynx in Europe (Lynx pardinus) (No. 111-115). Council of Europe.*

Ewer, R. F. 1973. *The carnivores. The World Naturalist, ed. Carrington, R. London: Weidenfeld and Nicolson.*

Fedriani, J. M.; Palomares, F.; and Delibes, M. 1999. *Niche relations among three sympatric Mediterranean carnivores. Oecologia, 121(1): 138-148. (Abstract only)*

Ferreras, P.; Rodríguez, A.; Palomares, F.; and Delibes, M. 2010. *Iberian lynx: the uncertain future of a critically endangered cat, in Biology and Conservation of Wild Felids, eds. Macdonald, D. W., and Loveridge, A. J., 511-524. Oxford: Oxford University Press.*

Fundación CBD-Habitat. 2019. *Censo de las poblaciones de lince ibérico 2018 (I): resultados. https://www.cbd-habitat.com/2019/08/06/censo-de-las-poblaciones-de-lince-iberico-2018-i-resultados/ Last accessed January 22, 2020.*

Hewitt, G. 2000. *The genetic legacy of the Quaternary ice ages. Nature, 405(6789): 907*

Johnson, W. E.; Eizirik, E.; Pecon-Slattery, J.; Murphy, W. J.; and others. 2006. *The Late Miocene Radiation of Modern Felidae: A Genetic Assessment. Science, 311:73-77.*

Kitchener, A. C.; Breitenmoser-Würsten, C.; Eizirik, E.; Gentry, A.; and others. 2017. *A revised taxonomy of the Felidae: The final report of the Cat Classification Task Force of the IUCN Cat Specialist Group. https://repository.si.edu/bitstream/handle/10088/32616/A_revised_Felidae_Taxonomy_CatNews.pdf*

Li, G.; Figueiró, H. V.; Eizirik, E.; and Murphy, W. J. 2019. *Recombination-aware phylogenomics reveals the structured genomic landscape of hybridizing cat species. Molecular biology and evolution, 36(10): 2111-2126.*

Macdonald, D. W.; Loveridge, A. J.; and Nowell, K. 2010b. *"Dramatis personae": An introduction to the wild felids, in Biology and Conservation of Wild Felids, eds. Macdonald, D. W., and Loveridge, A. J., 3-58. Oxford: Oxford University Press.*

O'Brien, S. J., and Johnson, W. E. 2007. *The evolution of cats. Scientific American. 297 (1):68-75.*

Rodríguez, A., and Calzada, J. 2015. *Lynx pardinus . The IUCN Red List of Threatened Species 2015: e.T12520A50655794. https://www.iucnredlist.org/species/12520/50655794 Last accessed January 7, 2020.*

Rodríguez-Varela, R.; Tagliacozzo, A.; Urena, I.; García, N.; and others. 2015. *Ancient DNA evidence of Iberian lynx palaeoendemism. Quaternary Science Reviews, 112: 172-180. (Abstract only)*

Simpson, G. G. 1944. *Tempo and Mode in Evolution. New York: Columbia University Press.*

Wildt, D. E.; Swanson, W.; Brown, J.; Sliwa, A.; and Vargas, A. 2010. *Felids ex situ: managed programmes, research and species recovery, in Biology and Conservation of Wild Felids, eds. Macdonald, D. W., and Loveridge, A. J., 217-235. Oxford: Oxford University Press.*

Zapata, S. C.; Travaini, A.; Ferreras, P.; and Delibes, M. 2007. *Analysis of trophic structure of two carnivore assemblages by means of guild identification. European Journal of Wildlife Research, 53(4): 276-286.*

Anderson, E., and Stebbins, Jr., G. L. *1954. Hybridization as an evolutionary stimulus. Evolution. 8(4): 378-388.*

Arnold, M. L. *2004. Transfer and origin of adaptations through natural hybridization: Were Anderson and Stebbins right? The Plant Cell. 16: 562-570.*

Barton, N. H., and Hewitt, G. M. *1985. Analysis of hybrid zones. Annual Review of Ecology and Systematics. 16:113-148.*

Culver, M.; Driscoll, C.; Eizirik, E.; and Spong, G. *2010. Genetic applications in wild felids, in Biology and Conservation of Wild Felids, ed. Macdonald, D. W., and Loveridge, A. J., 107-124. Oxford: Oxford University Press.*

Driscoll, C. A.; Menotti-Raymond, M.; Roca, A. I.; Hupe, K.; and others. *2007. The Near Eastern origin of cat domestication. Science. 317: 519-522.*

Driscoll, C.; Yamaguchi, N.; O'Brien, S. J.; and Macdonald, D. W. *2011. A suite of genetic markers useful in assessing wildcat (Felis silvestris ssp.) - domestic cat (Felis silvestris catus) admixture. Journal of Heredity. 102(SI): S87-S90.*

Encyclopaedia Britannica. *n.d. Wildcat, mammal, Felis silvestris. https://www.britannica.com/animal/wildcat-mammal-Felis-silvestris*

Ewer, R. F. *1973. The carnivores. The World Naturalist, ed. Carrington, R. London: Weidenfeld and Nicolson.*

Heptner, V. G., and Sludskii, A. A. *1972. Mammals of the Soviet Union, volume II, part 2: Carnivora (hyaenas and cats). Moscow: Vysshaya Shkola Publishers. English translation by Rao, P., 1992. General editor: Kothekar, V. S. New Delhi: Amerind Publishing. https://archive.org/details/mammalsofsov221992gept*

Herbst, M. *2009. Behavioural ecology and population genetics of the African wild cat, Felis silvestris Forster 1870, in the southern Kalahari. Doctoral dissertation, University of Pretoria.*

Hewitt, G. *2000. The genetic legacy of the Quaternary ice ages. Nature, 405(6789): 907*

Johnson, W. E.; Eizirik, E.; Pecon-Slattery, J.; Murphy, W. J.; and others. *2006. The Late Miocene Radiation of Modern Felidae: A Genetic Assessment. Science, 311:73-77.*

Kitchener, A. C.; Van Valkenburgh, B.; and Yamaguchi, N. *2010. Felid form and function, in Biology and Conservation of Wild Felids, ed. Macdonald, D. W., and Loveridge, A. J., 83-106. Oxford: Oxford University Press.*

Kitchener, A. C.; Breitenmoser-Würsten, C.; Eizirik, E.; Gentry, A.; and others. *2017. A revised taxonomy of the Felidae: The final report of the Cat Classification Task Force of the IUCN Cat Specialist Group. https://repository.si.edu/bitstream/handle/10088/32616/A_revised_Felidae_Taxonomy_CatNews.pdf*

Kurtén, B. *1965. On the evolution of the European wild cat, Felis silvestris Schreber. Acta Zoologica Fennica. 111:3-29.*

Li, G.; Davis, B. W.; Eizirik, E.; and Murphy, W. J. *2016. Phylogenomic evidence for ancient hybridization in the genomes of living cats (Felidae). Genome Research, 26(1): 1-11.*

Macdonald, D. W.; Loveridge, A. J.; and Nowell, K. *2010a. Dramatis personae: An introduction to the wild felids, in Biology and Conservation of Wild Felids, eds. Macdonald, D. W., and Loveridge, A. J., 3-58. Oxford: Oxford University Press.*

Macdonald, D. W.; Yamaguchi, N.; Kitchener, A. C.; Daniels, M.; and others. *2010b. Reversing cryptic extinction: the history, present, and future of the Scottish wildcat, in Biology and Conservation of Wild Felids, ed. Macdonald, D. W. and Loveridge, A. J., 471-491. Oxford: Oxford University Press.*

Mallet, J. *2005. Hybridization as an invasion of the genome. Trends in Ecology and Evolution. 20(5):229-237.*

Mattucci, F.; Oliveira, R.; Lyons, L. A.; Alves, P. C.; and Randi, E. *2016. European wildcat populations are subdivided into five main biogeographic groups: consequences of Pleistocene climate changes or recent anthropogenic fragmentation?. Ecology and Evolution, 6(1); 3-22.*

Nyakatura, K., and Bininda-Emonds, O. R. P. 2012. *Updating the evolutionary history of Carnivora (Mammalia): a new species-level supertree complete with divergence time estimates. BMC Biology. 10:12.*

O'Brien, S. J., and Johnson, W. E. 2007. *The evolution of cats. Scientific American. 297 (1):68-75.*

Steyer, K.; Kraus, R. H.; Mölich, T.; Anders, O.; and others. 2016. *Large-scale genetic census of an elusive carnivore, the European wildcat (Felis s. silvestris). Conservation Genetics. 17(5):1183-1199.*

Werdelin, L.; Yamaguchi, N.; Johnson, W. E.; and O'Brien, S. J. 2010. *Phylogeny and evolution of cats (Felidae), in Biology and Conservation of Wild Felids, eds. Macdonald, D. W., and Loveridge, A. J., 59-82. Oxford: Oxford: University Press.*

Wikipedia. 2019. *European wildcat. https://en.wikipedia.org/wiki/European_wildcat Last accessed May 8, 2019.*

Yamaguchi, N.; Kitchener, A. C.; Ward, J. M.; Driscoll, C. A.; and Macdonald, D. W. 2004. *Craniological differentiation between European wildcats (Felis silvestris silvestris), African wildcats (F. s. lybica) and Asian wildcats (F. s. ornata): implications for their evolution and conservation. Biological Journal of the Linnean Society, 83:47-63.*

Yamaguchi, N.; Kitchener, A.; Driscoll, C.; and Nussberger, B. 2015. *Felis silvestris. The IUCN Red List of Threatened Species 2015:e.T60354712A50652361.*

Cat Specialist Group. *2019. Chinese mountain cat. http://www.catsg.org/index.php?id=104 Last accessed December 24, 2019.*

He, L.; García-Perea, R.; Li, M.; and Wei, *F. 2004. Distribution and conservation status of the endemic Chinese mountain cat Felis bieti. Oryx, 38(1): 55-61.*

Johnson, W. E.; Eizirik, E.; Pecon-Slattery, J.; Murphy, W. J.; and others. *2006. The Late Miocene Radiation of Modern Felidae: A Genetic Assessment. Science, 311:73-77.*

Kitchener, A. C.; Breitenmoser-Würsten, C.; Eizirik, E.; Gentry, A.; and others. *2017. A revised taxonomy of the Felidae: The final report of the Cat Classification Task Force of the IUCN Cat Specialist Group. https://repository.si.edu/bitstream/handle/10088/32616/A_revised_Felidae_Taxonomy_CatNews.pdf*

Macdonald, D. W.; Yamaguchi, N.; Kitchener, A. C.; Daniels, M.; and others. *2010. Reversing cryptic extinction: the history, present, and future of the Scottish wildcat, in Biology and Conservation of Wild Felids, ed. Macdonald, D. W. and Loveridge, A. J., 471-491. Oxford: Oxford University Press.*

O'Brien, S. J., and Johnson, W. E. *2007. The evolution of cats. Scientific American. 297 (1):68-75.*

Riordan, P.; Sanderson, J.; Bao, W.; Abdukadir, A.; and Shi, K. *2015. Felis bieti . The IUCN Red List of Threatened Species 2015: e.T8539A50651398. https://www.iucnredlist.org/species/8539/50651398 Last accessed December 24, 2019.*

Sunquist, M. and Sunquist, F. *2002. Wild Cats of the World. Chicago and London: University of Chicago Press. Retrieved from https://play.google.com/store/books/details?id=IF8nDwAAQBAJ*

Tibet Nature Environmental Conservation Network. *2014. Chinese mountain cat. http://www.tibetnature.net/en/chinese-mountain-cat/ Last accessed December 24, 2019.*

Wikipedia. *2019. Chinese mountain cat. https://en.wikipedia.org/wiki/Chinese_mountain_cat Last accessed December 24, 2019.*

Cat Specialist Group. 2019. *African wildcat. http://www.catsg.org/index.php?id=112 Last accessed May 8, 2019.*

___. 2019. *Asiatic wildcat. http://www.catsg.org/index.php?id=102 Last accessed May 8, 2019.*

Driscoll, C.; Yamaguchi, N.; O'Brien, S. J.; and Macdonald, D. W. 2011. *A suite of genetic markers useful in assessing wildcat (Felis silvestris ssp.) - domestic cat (Felis silvestris catus) admixture. Journal of Heredity, 102(SI): S87-S90.*

Ewer, R. F. 1973. *The carnivores. The World Naturalist, ed. Carrington, R. London: Weidenfeld and Nicolson.*

Ghoddousi, A.; Hamidi, A. K.; Ghadirian, T.; and Assadi, S. B. 2016. *The status of wildcat in Iran-a crossroad of subspecies. Cat News S, 10: 60-63.*

Hu, Y.; Hu, S.; Wang, W.; Wu, X.; and others. 2014. *Earliest evidence for commensal processes of cat domestication. Proceedings of the National Academy of Sciences, USA. 111(1):116-120.*

Kitchener, A. C.; Breitenmoser-Würsten, C.; Eizirik, E.; Gentry, A.; and others. 2017. *A revised taxonomy of the Felidae: The final report of the Cat Classification Task Force of the IUCN Cat Specialist Group. https://repository.si.edu/bitstream/handle/10088/32616/A_revised_Felidae_Taxonomy_CatNews.pdf*

Macdonald, D. W.; Yamaguchi, N.; Kitchener, A. C.; Daniels, M.; and others. 2010a. *Reversing cryptic extinction: the history, present, and future of the Scottish wildcat, in Biology and Conservation of Wild Felids, ed. Macdonald, D. W. and Loveridge, A. J., 471-491. Oxford: Oxford University Press.*

Macdonald, D. W.; Loveridge, A. J.; and Nowell, K. 2010b. *Dramatis personae: An introduction to the wild felids, in Biology and Conservation of Wild Felids, eds. Macdonald, D. W., and Loveridge, A. J., 3-58. Oxford: Oxford University Press.*

Rhymer, J. M., and Simberloff, D. 1996. *Extinction by hybridization and introgression. Annual Review of Ecology and Systematics. 27:83-109.*

de Satgé, J.; Teichman, K.; and Cristescu, B. 2017. Competition and coexistence in a small carnivore guild. Oecologia, 184(4): 873-884.

Sliwa, A.; Herbst, M.; and Mills, M. 2010. *Black-footed cats (Felis nigripes) and African wild cats (Felis silvestris): a comparison of two small felids from South African arid lands, in Biology and Conservation of Wild Felids, ed. Macdonald, D. W., and Loveridge, A. J., 537-558.*

Sunquist, M. and Sunquist, F. 2002. *Wild Cats of the World. Chicago and London: University of Chicago Press. Retrieved from https://play.google.com/store/books/details?id=IF8nDwAAQBAJ*

Vigne, J. D.; Evin, A.; Cucchi, T.; Dai, L.; and others. 2016. *Earliest " domestic" cats in China identified as leopard cat (Prionailurus bengalensis). PloS One. 11(1):e0147295.*

Wikipedia. 2019. *African wildcat. https://en.wikipedia.org/wiki/African_wildcat Last accessed May 8, 2019.*

Wright, M., and Walters, S. 1980. *The Book of the Cat. New York: Summit Books.*

Yamaguchi, N.; Kitchener, A. C.; Ward, J. M.; Driscoll, C. A.; and Macdonald, D. W. 2004. *Craniological differentiation between European wildcats (Felis silvestris silvestris), African wildcats (F. s. lybica) and Asian wildcats (F. s. ornata): implications for their evolution and conservation. Biological Journal of the Linnean Society, 83:47-63.*

Yamaguchi, N.; Kitchener, A.; Driscoll, C.; and Nussberger, B. 2015. *Felis silvestris. The IUCN Red List of Threatened Species 2015:e.T60354712A50652361*

Driscoll, C. A.; Menotti-Raymond, M.; Roca, A. I.; Hupe, K.; and others. 2007. *The Near Eastern origin of cat domestication. Science, 317: 519-522.*

Driscoll, C.; Yamaguchi, N.; O'Brien, S. J.; and Macdonald, D. W. 2011. *A suite of genetic markers useful in assessing wildcat (Felis silvestris ssp.) - domestic cat (Felis silvestris catus) admixture. Journal of Heredity, 102(SI): S87-S90.*

Gentry, A.; Clutton-Brock, J.; and Groves, C. P. 2004. *The naming of wild animal species and their domestic derivatives. Journal of Archaeological Science, 31(5): 645-651.*

International Commission on Zoological Nomenclature. 2003. *Opinion 2027 (Case 3010), usage of 17 specific names based on wild species which are pre-dated by or contemporary with those based on domestic animals (Lepidoptera, Osteichthyes, Mammalia): Conserved. Bulletin of Zoological Nomenclature, 60: 81-84.*

Johnson, W. E.; Eizirik, E.; Pecon-Slattery, J.; Murphy, W. J.; and others. 2006. *The Late Miocene Radiation of Modern Felidae: A Genetic Assessment. Science, 311:73-77.*

Kitchener, A. C.; Breitenmoser-Würsten, C.; Eizirik, E.; Gentry, A.; and others. 2017. *A revised taxonomy of the Felidae: The final report of the Cat Classification Task Force of the IUCN Cat Specialist Group. https://repository.si.edu/bitstream/handle/10088/32616/A_revised_Felidae_Taxonomy_CatNews.pdf*

Macdonald, D. W.; Yamaguchi, N.; Kitchener, A. C.; Daniels, M.; and others. 2010. *Reversing cryptic extinction: the history, present, and future of the Scottish wildcat, in Biology and Conservation of Wild Felids, ed. Macdonald, D. W., and Loveridge, A. J., 471-491. Oxford: Oxford University Press.*

O'Brien, S. J., and Johnson, W. E. 2007. *The evolution of cats. Scientific American. 297 (1):68-75.*

de Queiroz, K. 2007. *Species concepts and species delimitation. Systematic Biology, 56(6): 879-886.*

Sunquist, M. and Sunquist, F. 2002. *Wild Cats of the World. Chicago and London: University of Chicago Press. Retrieved from https://play.google.com/store/books/details?id=IF8nDwAAQBAJ*

Turner, A., and Antón, M. 1997. *The Big Cats and Their Fossil Relatives: An Illustrated Guide to Their Evolution and Natural History. New York: Columbia University Press.*

Wikipedia. 2018. *International Code of Zoological Nomenclature. https://en.wikipedia.org/wiki/International_Code_of_Zoological_Nomenclature Last accessed November 25, 2018.*

___. 2018. *Opinion 2027. https://en.wikipedia.org/wiki/Opinion_2027 Last accessed November 25, 2018.*

Yamaguchi, N.; Kitchener, A.; Driscoll, C.; and Nussberger, B. 2015. *Felis silvestris. The IUCN Red List of Threatened Species, 2015:e.T60354712A50652361.*

In addition, references used in my two eBooks on house cats at https://www.amazon.com/s?i=digital-text&rh=p_27%3AB.+J.+Deming&s=relevancerank&text=B.+J.+Deming&ref=dp_byline_sr_ebooks_1 .